This book is, quite simply, brilliant. Readers wi'' ... ot-on reminders that God absolutely knew what He was doing when ... nsitive and strong people. If you have ever been called ... ver felt defective because of it, this empowering ...

Jennifer D ... and *The Happiness Dare*

Denise and Cheri's passion t ... ver the surprising strengths of their tender hearts, combined ... al stories they share, matched with actionable ideas, give women a v ... and the courage to flourish. Tender hearts will be lifted, strengthened, and freed.

Bonnie Gray, author of *Whispers of Rest*

I'm thrilled to finally have a biblically grounded book I can give someone who is an HSP or who loves an HSP, confident that they'll find solid information, practical guidance, and a new sense of freedom and acceptance as they no-doubtedly inhale this amazing resource.

Kathi Lipp, bestselling author and speaker

It's been a game changer to discover that my husband and one of our daughters are Highly Sensitive Persons. If you, too, have an HSP in your family (and the odds are you do!), *Sensitive and Strong* is your go-to guide. Denise and Cheri help you understand your HSP's unique wiring, accept them for who God created them to be, and appreciate how their perspective enriches your life.

Jill Savage, author of *No More Perfect Moms* and *No More Perfect Marriages*

As an HSP I appreciate that Denise and Cheri go beyond biology to address every part of who we are—psychological, emotional, social, and, most of all, spiritual. It's powerful to know God made HSPs intentionally and with a purpose.

Holley Gerth, counselor, life coach, and bestselling author of *You're Already Amazing*

If you are an HSP, this book is a must read. Not only will it help you feel less alone, but it will also give you practical tools, suggestions, and encouragement to thrive as a highly sensitive person.

Crystal Paine, *New York Times* bestselling author and founder of MoneySavingMom.com

Reading Cheri and Denise's honest stories and gentle wisdom feels like sitting with two empathetic mentors and realizing, *Finally, women who get it and are setting examples that I want to follow*. This is a book that I plan to keep within reach.

Jeanette Hanscome, author of *Suddenly Single Mom*

This book is a transformational handbook specifically for HSPs who want to cultivate a growth mindset, recognize their superpower(s), and serve God with their inherent gifting.

Chris Moss, author, speaker, and founder of Mentor Prep Academy

In a culture where sensitivity is synonymous with weakness, *Sensitive and Strong* is the battle cry of the deep feeler. The empathy and honest revelation within these pages allowed me to discover the strength in my own reactivity and embrace my natural wiring as a gift from God.

Jennifer Bryant, PracticalFamily.org

Cheri and Denise lead us to what's truly essential for our HSP lives. *Sensitive and Strong* is more than a prescription for self-care. It's a holistic plan to make our lives matter by reaching out to others with our unique wiring.

Amy Carroll, Proverbs 31 Ministries speaker and writer, author of *Breaking Up with Perfect* and *Exhale*

In *Sensitive and Strong*, Denise and Cheri gently guide the reader from accepting the beauty of how God uniquely created them to demonstrating how this sensitivity can be used as a super power for God and for good. What a beautiful gift.

Jenn Buell, TED Talk presenter and blogger at jennbuell.com

If you grew up hearing "you're too sensitive," you'll find kindred spirits in Cheri Gregory and Denise Hughes. *Sensitive and Strong* provides an eye-opening catalyst for recognizing whether or not you are an HSP. But it doesn't leave you with that label: Cheri and Denise help you replace negative reactions with intentional healthy choices, providing memorable examples and biblical suggestions for when you feel overwhelmed.

Gretchen Louise, founder of Kindred Grace

Whether you rejoice in your highly sensitive status or reject it, Denise and Cheri understand! They share science that shows how God created you and offer practical advice so you can live your life glorifying God and loving others, while honoring who you are.

Kendra Burrows, college instructor and blogger

Sensitive & Strong

Denise J. Hughes
and Cheri Gregory

HARVEST HOUSE PUBLISHERS
EUGENE, OREGON

Sensitive and Strong
Copyright © 2019 by Denise J. Hughes and Cheri Gregory
Published by Harvest House Publishers
Eugene, Oregon 97408
www.harvesthousepublishers.com

ISBN 978-0-7369-6923-9 (pbk)
ISBN 978-0-7369-6924-6 (eBook)

Library of Congress Cataloging-in-Publication Data

Names: Hughes, Denise J., author.
Title: Sensitive and strong / Denise J. Hughes and Cheri Gregory.
Description: Eugene : Harvest House Publishers, 2019. | Includes
    bibliographical references.
Identifiers: LCCN 2019014960 (print) | LCCN 2019022307 (ebook) | ISBN
    9780736969239 (pbk.)
Subjects: LCSH: Personality--Religious aspects--Christianity. | Sensitivity
    (Personality trait)--Religious aspects--Christianity. |
    Introversion--Religious aspects--Christianity. | Introverts--Religious
    life.
Classification: LCC BV4597.57 .H84 2019 (print) | LCC BV4597.57 (ebook) |
    DDC 248.4--dc23
LC record available at https://lccn.loc.gov/2019014960
LC ebook record available at https://lccn.loc.gov/2019022307

Printed in the United States of America

19 20 21 22 23 24 25 26 27 / BP-RD / 10 9 8 7 6 5 4 3 2 1

For those who feel
more sensitive
than most.

Contents

Part Two~Looking Up

Part Three~Looking Out

Foreword

*G*od, *why am I this way? Why is my heart wide-open to the hurts and disappointments of others? Why do I find myself moved by their pain? Why am I more prone to contemplative introspection than to spontaneity? Why is risk-taking not woven into my DNA? Is this all part of your divine plan for my life, or is it a genetic disposition I will forever battle to correct?*

I'm hesitant to admit how many times I've had this conversation with God. It permeated most of my college years and was still a running commentary when I entered medical school. On this particular morning, I arrived early at the hospital with the other medical students. We looked the same in our identical short white coats, but the myriad personalities spanned from the overconfident to the cautious. Our job was to gather clinical data on our assigned patient and prepare to present a treatment plan in front of the medical team.

Hospital rounds are the backbone of the medical education system. It is a place of teaching as well as excruciating correction. It is where you discover in the presence of your peers everything you've done right and everything you should have done better. It is a place where weakness is not welcome and emotions are kept in check. For me the goal was to conceal any evidence of sensitivity.

The team surrounded my patient's bed as I gave my report. After five minutes of rapid-fire questions, I received a nod from the chief resident indicating I had passed this morning's test. As the group exited the room, I reached for the pitcher of water sitting on my patient's table to fill her cup. Before I could shut her door, his words sliced through me. "Are you here to be a doctor or a nurse?"

My chest tightened. I had no idea what I had done to bring on this line of questioning. I passed the intellectual test but had still fallen short in his eyes. For the next few minutes, he lamented over how my job is not to fill water glasses and why I should not get attached to patients. His words flooded me. I couldn't breathe. All I could hear was the accelerated beating of my heart and the echo of my self-doubts reaffirming that being sensitive was a curse.

I refused to cry. I was not going to allow him to see he had wounded me with his words. His criticism mimicked the questions I place before God about why he made me this way.

The attending physician watched the exchange. He didn't join in the verbal beating, nor did he come to my defense. He signaled for the group to move on to the next patient. For the remainder of rounds, my mind disengaged from the conversations. My only thought was how I wished I could be different. I wanted to anesthetize my empathy and to become immune to the hurts of others. I wanted to replace the sensitive side of my personality with a heart that felt less and a consciousness that was oblivious to unmet needs.

I prepared for late afternoon rounds robotically. My patient was the last one of the day. I reported on how she had progressed and shared the most recent lab data. The chief resident nodded in agreement, and I turned toward the door. Before I could exit the room, he quipped, "You don't want to refill her water again?" The room went silent except for the sound of water flowing.

Standing at the side of her bed, the attending physician was pouring from the pitcher into her cup. He leaned in to speak to the patient and then ushered our team out of her room. Once in the hospital corridor, he turned to face me and asked, "Explain to the group the rationale behind why you gave her water this morning."

In one long exhalation, the words released. I shared how I noticed the dryness of her lips and how she repeatedly licked them during her conversation with the group. I explained seeing her glance over at the water while we discussed her case. While observing her interaction with the medical team, I noticed her reluctance to ask questions and how she apologized for being trouble whenever asking the staff to do the most basic things for her. "I knew she wouldn't ring the buzzer for the nurse to fill the water, so I filled it."

The next words the attending physician spoke forever changed how I viewed sensitivity. "You perceived what was *not* being said. This is a quality many take years in medicine to develop, but for some it is a gift from above."

For the first time, I saw sensitivity not as a weakness but as an opportunity for God to use me in a unique way. It allowed me to cease asking God to change me and instead ask him to reveal to me how I am designed to accomplish his purpose for my life.

Cheri and Denise understand the complexity of living life as a Highly Sensitive Person (HSP). They tackle the misconceptions of HSPs being ineffective, highly emotionally, fragile, and weary with a balanced look at how HSPs are wired. During my interview on the Grit and Grace podcast, Cheri's comments on sensory overload and the need for intentional sensory downtime relayed her intimate knowledge of the topic. Much like Denise, *sensitive* is a word I have resisted including in my list of character traits, but I am learning the trait is a gift I must be willing to unwrap.

I challenge every person who has ever wished they were less sensitive to read this book. Let it reveal to you both the challenges and the rewards of being an HSP. Let it show you how to tap into your unique strengths. Let it confirm you can be both sensitive and strong.

Saundra Dalton-Smith, MD
Board-certified internal medicine physician and author of *Sacred Rest*

Introduction

The Tale of Two HSPs
It Really Is a Thing

Denise's Story

I hated Easter Sunday, which made me feel guilty because Mom said it was the most important Sunday of the year. For me, it was the worst. I couldn't understand why we had to celebrate the resurrection of our Lord by wearing itchy ruffled dresses and tightly buckled patent leather shoes. And that's to say nothing of those matching straw hats with that awful elastic band squeezing my chin. Such outfits were the bane of Easter Sunday.

After raising two boys, my mom was elated to finally have a little girl she could doll up in pretty dresses, but I'm told I was a temperamental baby, always fidgety and restless inside anything with lace. As a toddler, I hid behind my mother's legs whenever we walked into an unfamiliar place, and as a preschooler, I stubbornly refused to dance or sing or do anything that resembled a performance in front of others.

"Shy." That's how most people described me, and they hoped I'd grow out of it someday.

On Easter morn, I sat on the hard wooden pew, squirming inside my special dress. Mom tried to bribe me with wintergreen-flavored Certs to sit still, but I didn't like wintergreen. Too minty, I argued. Mom just shook her head at her perplexing daughter.

After the service, the congregation sauntered onto the patio where they basked in the sunlight while visiting with friends. From behind my mother's skirt, I shielded my eyes from the noonday brightness and watched as the other girls twirled in their Easter finest. I liked the way their waist-high sashes trailed them with a final swoosh, but my own sash had bothered me all morning. First, Mom had tied it too tightly, so I tried to retie it, but after several attempts my satin bow merely limped along behind me.

I wished I could spin in the sunlight and relish the flourish of satin and lace like the other girls, but all I wanted to do was go home and put on something comfortable. I felt certain something was wrong with me, but I didn't know what it was or how to fix it or if it was even fixable.

Cheri's Story

The preacher held up his Bible and shouted into the microphone. "How many of you have heard that God loves you just the way you are?"

As I smiled and raised a hand, the preacher's booming voice caused the sound system to emit a deafening high-pitched squeal. I plugged my ears, but not fast enough to prevent the stabbing pain. I closed my eyes, massaged my temples, and took a deep breath.

"You may have heard that God loves you just the way you are," the preacher bellowed, pounding the pulpit for emphasis, "but I am here to tell you the truth tonight: God does not love you just the way you are!"

My eyes flew open. My hands dropped to my lap. My breathing stopped. And my ears began to buzz. *Cheri*, I said to myself, *get a grip.* I tried to take a slow deep breath, but all I could do was gasp while the buzzing in my ears grew louder. *You know what he's trying to say. He's preaching against "cheap grace."* The cavernous room with 5,000 people faded away as the buzzing filled my head. *Logically, you know that God loves you too much to leave you where you are.* But even as I fought to stay rational, the preacher's words "God does not love you" repeated on autoplay inside my head. A rogue wave of emotion engulfed me. *You are 40 years old. Hold yourself together. Don't make a scene.*

But it was too late. Feeling like the one truth that kept my heart beating had been ripped right out, I covered my face with my hands and sobbed like an inconsolable child. My bewildered husband sat stiffly, gazing intently forward. In the car on the way home, he asked, "What set you off this time?" As I tried to explain, he shook his head.

"You overreacted. You were the only one there who heard it that way." I would love to report that this was a one-time incident, but I have a long history of overreacting in response to overstimulation.

Almost but Not Quite

Years later, we (Denise and Cheri) met at a writers' conference. Over the course of several conversations, we discovered we not only shared a love for Jesus and a passion for writing, but also something else. Separately, we have long studied the various personality frameworks: the Myers-Briggs Types, the Keirsey-Bates Temperaments, the Clifton Strengths-Finder, the Enneagram, the Fascination Advantage System, and the Five Love Languages. These frameworks provide a way to recognize and name common human experiences. They give us a shared language for better understanding ourselves and how we can relate to others and the world around us.

Arguably, the most predominant feature of any known temperament assessment is the field of introversion and extroversion. An extrovert is often described as talkative, deriving energy by being around people. As natural "people persons," they're externally oriented to the world around them. By contrast, an introvert is often described as quiet, deriving energy through times of solitude. As natural listeners and observers, they're internally oriented toward introspection and reflection.

One of us is a true-blue introvert—Denise—and one of us is an extrovert—Cheri. For both of us, however, none of the personality frameworks—not even the oft-described polarity of introversion and extroversion—have been able to explain a significant factor in both of our lives.

Putting a Name to It

One day we met for lunch at Cheesecake Factory and enjoyed a long conversation about all things writing, publishing, and books. Always books.

"Have you read *Quiet* by Susan Cain?" Cheri asked.

"Yes! I admit I approached it with some skepticism. I didn't think there was anything new I could learn about introversion, but that section on physiology was a game-changer."

"Yep, same here. Except it's not just about introverts. Extroverts experience it, too."

What was so revelatory in this section of Susan Cain's book? Cain went beyond the typical analysis of temperaments and dove into the science—the physiology of what's been called "high reactivity" by some and "Sensory Processing Sensitivity" (SPS) by others. When Cain discusses Jerome Kagan's work in observing children exposed to different kinds of stimulating environments, she notes that some children were "'high reactive'—to new sights, sounds, and smells."[1] In other words, some children reacted more visibly when they heard loud noises or smelled strong odors. Infants as young as four months old "thrashed their arms like punk rockers" in response to the stimuli.[2] This high reactivity is attributed to a more reactive amygdala, which "serves as the brain's emotional switchboard, receiving information from the senses and then signaling the rest of the brain and nervous system how to respond."[3] Basically, the differences in the way children process external stimuli can be observed in infants as young as four months of age.

In her groundbreaking book *Quiet*, Cain goes on to say that what Jerome Kagan calls "high reactivity," Elaine Aron calls "sensitivity."[4] After years of researching Sensory Processing Sensitivity (SPS), psychologist Elaine Aron concludes that approximately 20 percent of the population experience a much higher degree of sensitivity in response to physical, social, and emotional stimuli. She coined the 20 percent as Highly Sensitive Persons or HSPs.[5] And the name stuck.

Today, the term Highly Sensitive Person (HSP) is the most widely used moniker for this common experience. It's considered common because one in five people experience this trait of sensory sensitivity. This trait is no respecter of persons either. It's found in both males and females, young and old, rich and poor. The trait is physiological—it's how a person is wired.

This newfound knowledge has been freeing for many HSPs who

spent years wondering why they respond to certain situations very differently than most of their counterparts. (Cheri is in this camp!) Knowing you're an HSP can help you understand how an overstimulating experience can be draining for you while invigorating for a non-HSP. Knowing you're an HSP can also help you navigate different kinds of stimulating environments with deftness, and it can help you choose your responses with wisdom when confronted with a taxing situation. Understanding the many positive implications of being an HSP is the goal of this book, and yet, the word "sensitive" has other connotations, too, some of which are less than positive.

In the context of being an HSP, "sensitive" means "responsive" to stimuli, reflecting a greater degree of awareness. You might call an HSP an HAP (Highly Aware Person) due to their highly responsive natures. But in typical American society, the word "sensitive" has other meanings as well. In some contexts, being sensitive implies being fragile or thin-skinned. Depending on your background or upbringing, to be called sensitive could be considered derogatory—a thing to avoid at all costs. In some social or familial circles, it's considered weak to be sensitive. For this reason, some people are reluctant to call themselves a Highly Sensitive Person, much less tell anyone else they're an HSP. (Denise is in this camp!)

Being an HSP, however, is not the same thing as being emotional or frail, which is why we've titled this book *Sensitive and Strong*. Being both "sensitive" and "strong" is part of an HSP's reality. We can be strong friends in relationships, strong partners in business, and strong members of communities. We can be strong for great causes, and we can be strong in hard times.

> TRUE SCIENTIFIC EXPLORATION CAN SERVE TO MAGNIFY THE WONDER AND BEAUTY OF GOD'S DESIGN FOR DIVERSITY AMONG HUMANITY.

In the pages that follow, we'll take a closer look at what it means to live with Sensory Processing Sensitivity. We'll touch on the science behind it, and these discussions about our genetic wiring will inevitably lead to important conversations about our Creator and his intentional design of each individual person. As believers in the God of the Bible, we are not afraid of scientific findings. We believe all truth is God's truth; therefore, if something is true, then it is true because God designed it to be so. God and science are not mutually exclusive. True scientific exploration can serve to magnify the wonder and beauty of God's design for diversity among humanity.

Sensitive and Strong serves as a guide for HSPs and those who love them. In *Part One: Looking In*, we'll examine the way God designed us, the way he "knit us" in our mother's womb (Psalm 139:13-14), and we'll consider how certain sensitivities can affect the way an HSP interacts with the world. In *Part Two: Looking Up*, we'll focus on some typical scenarios that HSPs face, and we'll work to navigate these various contexts by looking first to Jesus, who is the source of our strength and the perfect example we should all seek to emulate. In *Part Three: Looking Out*, we'll explore the ways the Spirit can guide sensitive souls to live with an outward focus, loving and serving others.

For the More Sensitive Than Most

While we first heard about Sensory Processing Sensitivity through Susan Cain's book *Quiet*, we've gone on to study and learn more about it. We are researchers and teachers, not counselors or clinicians. This is the story of our journey through discovery and growth, and we invite you to join us. If you see either yourself or someone you know in these pages, our hope is that you will begin to embrace the ways an HSP can be both sensitive and strong.

As we have talked with hundreds of sensitive sisters, we've noticed a consistent theme. Many have heard dismissive comments like these:

- "Why do you have to be like that?"
- "You're just too sensitive."
- "Just relax and forget about it."
- "Don't let things get to you."

If that's you, we're here to tell you it's okay. In fact, a highly sensitive nature also correlates with certain strengths you can offer the world around you.

In the chapters that follow, we'll help you to:

- discover you're different, not defective
- understand your genetic disposition to an over-abundance of stimuli
- see how your sensitivities correlate to key strengths
- respond to stressful situations with confidence and calm
- harness your strengths to serve others

> YOU CAN EMBRACE THE VERY THINGS THAT MAKE YOU UNIQUE AND COME TO SEE YOURSELF AS SENSITIVE *AND* STRONG.

That day we had lunch at Cheesecake Factory, we realized we're both HSPs, but we have different sensitivities. The things that might drive one of us crazy won't really bother the other one, and vice versa. We also realized that one of us (Cheri) was thrilled to discover she's an HSP while the other (Denise) would rather crawl under a rock than call herself sensitive. Despite these differences, we are both convinced you don't have to wrestle with Easter dresses or distressing messages. You don't have to be overly stimulated or easily overwhelmed. You can embrace the very things that make you unique and come to see yourself as sensitive *and* strong.

Part One

Looking In

Yet you, LORD, are our Father.
We are the clay, you are the potter;
we are all the work of your hand.

ISAIAH 64:8

1

The First Step in the Journey
Taking the HSP Quiz
Denise

I wanted to do something different this year for my grown daughter's birthday. Instead of finding something to wrap in a box, I wanted to find a way she and I could have more shared experiences. This has been a challenge because we are so different in our temperaments and personalities. I'm the quiet, bookish type, and my daughter is a vivacious spirit, full of life and always looking for a new place to visit or a new sight to see. Finding activities we can do together—that we would both enjoy—can be tricky, so this year I purchased tickets to a Carrie Underwood concert, knowing we both enjoyed her music.

Outside the Staples Center in downtown Los Angeles, my daughter and I followed the throng of people from the parking lot to the nearest entrance, where everyone filed into a long line for the security check. My daughter was visibly excited, which made my mom-heart glad, but then I noticed the signs posted along the walkway. The signs said something to the effect of *WARNING: If you are pregnant or have heart problems, this performance will include smoking machines, pyrotechnic displays, and strobe lighting effects.* They were the kind of signs you see when you're in line for a high-speed roller coaster at an amusement park, so I took a deep breath and prepared myself for a highly stimulating concert.

The concert delivered everything the signs promised and more:

loud speakers, thick smoke, bright lights, and indoor fireworks. I felt myself growing more tired by the minute while my sweet daughter soaked up every sound and strobe light. Then, at one point the concert slowed, the lights dimmed, and all the other musicians left the stage. Carrie Underwood sat atop the grand piano and sang a ballad with the accompaniment of the pianist. It was beautiful. I savored this sweet respite and remembered why I enjoyed Carrie's music so much.

Later that night, when I could finally crawl into the comfort of my soft bed, I smiled at the memory of my daughter's face so full of joy. We had shared something together, and that made everything worthwhile, even though I knew I'd be comatose the next day. Because for me, I need some down time to recover from such a highly stimulating event, whereas my daughter would likely wake up the following morning energized and ready for a new day.

Been There, Done That

For a long time, I wondered why I couldn't enjoy the same things other people seemed to. Why couldn't I enjoy the same concert that thousands of other people obviously did? Why am I so different?

> ONE IN FIVE PEOPLE ARE HSPs, BUT MANY
> HAVE BECOME GOOD AT HIDING IT.

If you relate more to my experience of the concert, it is possible you're an HSP, too. If you relate more to my daughter's experience of the concert, then it is at least likely you have a close relative or friend who is an HSP. Since one in five people are HSPs, you probably know quite a few, but many have become good at hiding it. Many HSPs try to blend in with everyone around them—like I did at the concert—but there's a cost to pay later, like spending the following day in a quiet stupor.

Have you ever been there, done that? Have you ever wondered why the same event can be so energizing for some yet exhausting for others, perhaps even you? Take the following quiz and find out!

Are You an HSP?

For each statement, circle 0 if the statement is rarely true of you, but circle 1 if the statement is almost always true of you.

1. I see my home as a place of refuge from a world that is often draining.
   Rarely Ever—Almost Always
   0   1

2. I quickly pick up on the moods of others in the room.
   Rarely Ever—Almost Always
   0   1

3. I like to spend time thinking about things.
   Rarely Ever—Almost Always
   0   1

4. Strong smells, like perfume and cologne, can give me a headache.
   Rarely Ever—Almost Always
   0   1

5. I have deep empathy for the suffering of others.
   Rarely Ever—Almost Always
   0   1

6. I take longer to process new information than most of my peers.
   Rarely Ever—Almost Always
   0   1

7. I avoid movies and TV shows that depict violence.
   Rarely Ever—Almost Always
   0   1

8. The beauty of my surroundings affects me in really positive ways.
   Rarely Ever—Almost Always
   0   1

9. I tend to notice things others miss.
    Rarely Ever—Almost Always
         0   1

10. When a loud noise startles me, it takes me longer to recover than most of my peers.
    Rarely Ever—Almost Always
         0   1

11. I devote considerable time to reflecting deeply on matters that are important to me.
    Rarely Ever—Almost Always
         0   1

12. I've been told I'm too sensitive.
    Rarely Ever—Almost Always
         0   1

13. I enjoy creative endeavors.
    Rarely Ever—Almost Always
         0   1

14. I seem to need more rest than most.
    Rarely Ever—Almost Always
         0   1

15. If there's going to be sunshine, I make sure I have my sunglasses with me.
    Rarely Ever—Almost Always
         0   1

16. I prefer one-on-one conversations to milling around a room full of people.
    Rarely Ever—Almost Always
         0   1

17. I find small-talk to be annoying.
    Rarely Ever—Almost Always
         0   1

18. When I feel overwhelmed, I recover best by finding a quiet room with low lighting.
Rarely Ever—Almost Always
0   1

19. I am slow to make decisions.
Rarely Ever—Almost Always
0   1

20. I can get easily lost in my thoughts.
Rarely Ever—Almost Always
0   1

21. I love the world of music and the arts.
Rarely Ever—Almost Always
0   1

22. Clutter is very distracting to me.
Rarely Ever—Almost Always
0   1

23. When I make a mistake, I tend to mull it over for a long time.
Rarely Ever—Almost Always
0   1

24. A sudden change of plans makes me feel disoriented and off-kilter.
Rarely Ever—Almost Always
0   1

25. When I hear about tragedies in the world, I can't shake the feeling I need to do something about it.
Rarely Ever—Almost Always
0   1

26. The intensity of my own emotions can surprise me at times.
Rarely Ever—Almost Always
0   1

27. I've been told I overthink things.
Rarely Ever—Almost Always
0   1

28. I enjoy the life of the mind.
Rarely Ever—Almost Always
0   1

29. I try to fit in by being more outgoing than I really am.
Rarely Ever—Almost Always
0   1

30. Repetitive noises, like a faucet dripping or a pen tapping, are very distracting to me.
Rarely Ever—Almost Always
0   1

31. I can experience the emotions of others almost as if they're my own.
Rarely Ever—Almost Always
0   1

32. Hunger can hijack my brain and make me hangry.
Rarely Ever—Almost Always
0   1

33. In public places, I often retreat to the bathroom to have a few minutes alone.
Rarely Ever—Almost Always
0   1

34. Itchy textures bother me, and I'm quick to cut the tags from new clothes.
Rarely Ever—Almost Always
0   1

35. I need down time to transition between activities.
Rarely Ever—Almost Always
0   1

36. Caffeine seems to affect me more than my peers.
    Rarely Ever—Almost Always
    0   1

37. The more I try to multitask, the more rattled or discombobulated I become.
    Rarely Ever—Almost Always
    0   1

38. I avoid performing under pressure.
    Rarely Ever—Almost Always
    0   1

39. I wonder how other people get so much done with so little effort.
    Rarely Ever—Almost Always
    0   1

40. I have a deep sense of right and wrong, of justice, and of fairness.
    Rarely Ever—Almost Always
    0   1

Okay, go back and tally your score. The closer your total is to 40, the more likely it is that you're an HSP. If your total is somewhere in the middle range (around 20) or lower, the less likely it is that you're an HSP.

If you're super interested, you can take a much more in-depth test at www.SensitiveAndStrongBook.com.

The reactions to discovering one is an HSP can vary. Some will find it fascinating while others will bemoan the very idea. We get it, so we've devoted a chapter to each response in chapters 2 and 3.

Where We Go from Here

Much of the literature on Highly Sensitive Persons (HSPs) does two things: 1) Provides a checklist or quiz to determine if you are an

HSP, and 2) provides a list of ways you can mitigate an overly stimulating world. In other words, once you know you're an HSP, they offer
some suggestions for how you can better care for your highly sensitive
nature. End of story.

> EVERY PERSON ON THIS PLANET, WHETHER AN HSP
> OR NOT, HAS AN ASSIGNMENT FROM HEAVEN.

As Christ-followers, though, we believe this two-part sequence fails
to account for God's call on our lives. We understand the initial need
to look inward and understand how we're wired (which is what we'll
do in Part One), as well as the need to look upward and learn how to
respond to our environments in healthy ways (which is what we'll do
in Part Two). But we also believe we are placed on this earth for a purpose greater than ourselves. We take the Apostle Paul at his word when
he said to the believers in Ephesus, "We are God's handiwork, created
in Christ Jesus to do good works, which God prepared in advance for
us to do" (Ephesians 2:10). Every person on this planet, whether an
HSP or not, has an assignment from heaven, and it involves living out-
wardly and investing in others.

Jesus summed it up best when he said that we are here to love God
and love others (Matthew 22:37-39). How we do that will look different for each of us, so if we're going to examine what it means to live as
an HSP, we want to do so with the aim to better love and serve those
in our respective spheres. In fact, we contend in this book that HSPs
can offer certain gifts to the world that their non-HSP counterparts
cannot, just as non-HSPs can offer gifts to the world that HSPs cannot. To this end, this book adds a much-needed third part to the discussions involving HSPs. In addition to looking in and looking up,
we will explore what it means to look out by considering the many
strengths of HSPs and the special ways they can contribute to the
world around them.

But first, here's a closer look at what you can expect in the rest of
Part One:

- In chapter 2, we'll discuss what it means to be an HSP.

- In chapter 3, we'll discuss what it does not mean to be an HSP and dispel some of the misconceptions that come with it.

- In chapter 4, we'll take a closer look at some of the science behind this genetic trait.

- In chapter 5, we'll examine both the advantages and the disadvantages to being an HSP.

- In chapter 6, we'll look at some of the unhealthy attitudes and behaviors HSPs can fall into if they're not careful.

- In chapter 7, we'll focus on how HSPs can flourish in positive and healthy ways with a growth mindset.

- In chapter 8, we'll explore the good news about HSPs.

Are you ready? Let's get started!

2

The Five Factors of Sensitivity

Appreciating What It Means to Be an HSP

Cheri

Hi, I'm Cheri. And I'm a self-improvement junkie.

I've always felt like the odd-one-out. Not just different; downright defective—which means I've spent most of my life trying to fix myself, paying for counseling and coaching, attending dozens of workshops and seminars...per year. Buying the entire self-help section of Barnes and Noble—all to no avail.

When I was just 16 years old, I attended a workshop that introduced me to the four basic temperaments: the fun-loving Sanguine, the detail-conscious Melancholy, the achievement-oriented Choleric, and the peace-keeping Phlegmatic. Initially, so many light bulbs went on as I gained vital insights into myself and my family members.

But the more I studied these personality types, the more questions I had. Something about me was off. No matter how hard I tried, I didn't fully fit the descriptions of my primary and secondary temperaments. My inner intensity switch seemed preset to "high" and wouldn't dial down, no matter how hard I tried. I truly loved people and parties...until they wore me out. I could take charge of any situation...until I got overwhelmed and dissolved into tears. I couldn't remember my own phone number—but couldn't forget harsh words I'd heard.

Even as I went on to teach personality workshops with outer

confidence, I berated myself inwardly for being an imposter. *You're just a wannabe. A failed extrovert. A fraud.*

When Change Won't Happen

What I longed to change about myself was this extra layer of intensity that I couldn't hide, no matter how hard I tried. I constantly felt "high maintenance"—like a burden to others and an enigma to myself. Well-meaning loved ones offered their best advice over the years:

- "Just stop overthinking things."
- "Just let go and let God."
- "Just don't take things so personally."
- "Just learn to r-e-l-a-x!"
- "Just don't be so hard on yourself."

Excellent bits of advice, every single one. But without the companion how-to manual (yes, I would buy *Emotional Contentment for Dummies* if someone were to write it) I could never figure out how to apply these well-intentioned clichés to my everyday life. What seemed so obvious to others felt unfathomable for me.

Turns out, I didn't need advice; what I needed was a map.

Finding the Map

Learning that I'm a Highly Sensitive Person was like finding that map and discovering that it's actually a treasure map with a big red X that says, "You are here. This is what's normal for you." As I read Susan Cain's *Quiet* and Elaine Aron's *The Highly Sensitive Person*, I peppered the pages with so much highlighting and so many notes of "This is me!" that it finally hit me: *There's nothing wrong with me. I'm a normal HSP.*

> THERE'S NOTHING WRONG WITH ME.
> I'M A NORMAL HSP.

An enormous sense of relief washed over me. In the space of a few short days, my life-long list of everything I needed to do to fix my defective self changed into a list of things I could stop doing.

- I could stop basing "normal" on everyone else's experiences.
- I could stop pretending to be someone I'm not.
- I could finally stop wondering, *What's wrong with me?*

You know how in the final moments of some Disney movies all the grim, gloomy grayness miraculously transforms into joyous, brilliant color? That's what happened inside of me. All of a sudden, so much of what had never made sense in my life now made total sense. It felt like a miracle when it happened. And it still feels like a miracle, six years later, each time I remember: *There's nothing wrong with me. I'm a normal HSP.*

What It Means to Be an HSP

What exactly does it mean to be an HSP? We're going to spend the rest of the book answering this very question. But let's start with a basic definition. Pioneer researcher Elaine Aron summarizes the core qualities of high sensitivity using the acronym D.O.E.S.:[1]

- Depth of processing
- Overstimulation
- Emotional reactivity and empathy
- Sensing the subtle

Here's what these mean for HSPs.

1. HSPs need time to process.

I've quit apologizing for being so slow. For not being a spontaneous "Ready. Fire! Aim." kind of gal or even a "Ready. Aim. Fire!" kind of gal. I tend to aim...aim...aim...aim...until frustrated friends and family are ready to "fire" me. To action-oriented people, I appear overly cautious, even fearful. But to me? I'm just taking the time I need to figure things out. I'm going through various possibilities, pondering the ramifications of choices. I'm taking time to connect the past with the present and the future, to recognize cause-and-effect. I'm developing theories and analyzing what went right, what went wrong, and how to do things different and better next time.

Turns out, there's a term for people who do these things: deep processors. I no longer feel stupid because I don't "think on my feet." I now know that it's normal for me, as an HSP, to need processing time before I can make sense of what's going on in my head. I used to feel pressured (and, frankly, baffled!) at staff meetings when a topic was suddenly introduced, minimally discussed, and then quickly brought to a vote. I usually abstained, feeling that no vote was better than an uninformed vote. But once I recognized that my need for reflection time was valid, I began to speak up. I realized that in a group of 40 people, I expressed the unspoken needs of 8-12 other adults who couldn't (or at least didn't) speak for themselves.

I started saying things like:

- "I move that the vote be scheduled three days from today for those who need time to consider the issue."

- "When a topic will be brought to vote, may we receive written information at least 72 hours in advance so we can come prepared with questions?"

- "I understand that many of us here are very comfortable with making decisions this quickly, but some of us are not. Some of us need a day or two before we can even start asking the right questions. To vote now would exclude input from people with important perspectives to offer."

This did not make me popular with some of my superiors. I did, however, receive grateful looks, whispered thank-yous, and emails of appreciation from fellow HSPs.

2. HSPs are easily overstimulated.

During my college summers, I worked in a law office. Every single day, about an hour before lunch, I found myself asking the same question: Why am I getting a headache? I'd tick through the usual considerations: Did I get enough sleep last night? Yes. Did I eat breakfast this morning? Yes. Have I drunk enough water? Yes, I have my water bottle right in front of me. Then I'd see the smoke wafting up from the cubicle across the hall. *Oh. That's why.*

I dreaded the walk to the Human Resources director's office, but it was either that or go home. I couldn't, despite my colleagues' unhelpful suggestions, "just ignore it." Contrary to judgmental comments, it wasn't "all in my head." And, contrary to suspicious speculations, I never sat and watched for the smoke to rise and then pretended to have a headache so I could get out of work.

First, I felt the pain. Next, I tried to figure out what was causing it. Finally, I found the environmental factor. Then I had to decide what to do about it. Yes, my HR director was supportive and asked my coworker to stop smoking every time I complained. (I'm not sure who was more relieved when second-hand smoke laws were enacted—her or me!) But I hated feeling so "high-maintenance." Nobody else in the law firm seemed to notice. Why did I? Did I have a hidden agenda against smokers? But it wasn't just smoke, I soon learned.

One of the defining characteristics of Highly Sensitive Persons is our heightened sensory perceptions. As a middle school teacher, I couldn't stand the smell of perfume or body spray. At home, I couldn't handle scented candles or trash bags with deodorizer or anything bearing the dreaded brand name: Febreze. I happen to be especially "scentsitive," and we'll explore all sensory sensitivities in more depth in chapter 5.

3. HSPs feel things intensely.

My father recalls, "As a young girl, in kindergarten and primary grades, you reacted immediately to me. If I simply moved my finger, you instantly knew what I meant and promptly changed what you were doing. At the slightest demonstration of my displeasure, you began to cry."

As I grew older, my skin did not grow any thicker. Negative events and emotions continued to affect me deeply. The Columbine High School shooting—which happened during my tenth year of teaching—shook me to my core. In the following days, I remember disciplining a student and then thinking, "Will she come back some day and shoot me for this?" My own children were seven and eight at the time, and I alternated between wondering, "How can I keep them from growing up to be school shooters?" and "How must the mothers of those two boys be feeling right now?" Daily, I caught myself scanning my classroom for safe places to hide and alternate exit routes. I was in graduate school at the time, and I wrote an entire research paper connecting the revenge theme in *Frankenstein* to the shootings. While most of my colleagues had "moved on," I continued reeling from the loss of innocence.

On the flip side, I also experience positive emotions intensely. My high school journals are filled with exuberant declarations of "I am so happy-ecstatic today!" and "This was the best day ever!" My gratitude journals chronicle the myriad experiences and relationships that have brought me real connection, true satisfaction, and genuine joy: the wonder of a sunset horseback ride on the beach, the side-splitting hilarity of watching comedy with my family, the precious hummingbirds that visit my five feeders.

My text messages with family and friends involve copious ALL CAPS, a decadent use of exclamation points (!!!!!!!!!!), and every imaginable happy-face emoji.

4. HSPs are highly empathetic.

One day when my daughter Annemarie was about four years old, I sent her to her room for a time-out. She made a huge scene as she dragged herself up the stairs, fake crying louder with each step. Nonplussed by her obvious theatrics, I sat on the couch to read a magazine until her time was up. But her HSP little brother Jonathon, 21 months younger and fiercely devoted, became distraught. With brow furrowed and lower lip out, he marched up to me and announced, "I have wuvved Am-a-wee all my wife!" Gesturing in helpless indignation, he added, "And you have made her cwy!" before melting into a puddle of misery. He could not bear that his beloved sister was in pain; as a Highly Sensitive Person, he felt it as his own.

HSP empathy is not limited to people we know. When I was in

eighth grade, a movie about the 1978 "Jonestown Massacre" was shown during a church youth group meeting. I don't remember why the movie was shown; what I do remember vividly is feeling devastated for the family members of the more than 900 people who had followed Jim Jones to their deaths. The movie made such an impact that I asked my father to take me back for a repeat showing. Although we didn't have the term "HSP" as part of our lingo, he understood me well enough to know that I needed him to empathize with my pain and help me process the enormity of it.

HSP empathy isn't even limited to people. One HSP friend recalls choosing black as her favorite color in kindergarten because nobody else picked it, and she didn't want it to feel unwanted. And she slept with each of her 33 stuffed animals in turn—even the giant dog with the glinting eyes that terrified her at night—because she wanted them all to feel equally loved.

5. HSPs notice nuances.

One evening, years before I knew about being an HSP, my husband and I were walking out of a restaurant toward the parking lot. As the conversation between a couple ahead of us grew louder, I told Daniel, "We need to give them lots of space."

He looked confused. "Why? They're talking and laughing!"

Just then, the woman reached down, took off her high heels, threw them at the man, and ran back into the restaurant crying.

Daniel looked at me baffled...and a bit scared. "How did you know?"

I couldn't explain to him how I had read the situation from the back. I had just known.

HSPs notice nuances in a wide variety of ways. When I'd hug and kiss my son good night when he was a little tyke, he could always guess what I'd been eating. He'd say, "I smell chocolate, Mama!" I'd jokingly reply, "You smell carrots!" And he'd shake his head knowingly. "No, Mama; you smell like chocolate!" earning himself the life-long nickname "Jiminy Cricket" (after the Disney character who served as Pinocchio's external conscience).

As an HSP, you pick up on things others might miss. At a musical concert, HSPs might pick up on the slightest change in tempo, pitch, or timbre. While enjoying a meal, HSPs may notice faint but distinctive differences in flavor, texture, and aroma. When writing a letter, an HSP might mull over word choices, seeking the precise shade of meaning she wants to communicate. HSPs might like to play with the lighting, temperature, colors, and fabrics in a room until they are "just right."

After a group discussion, an HSP might seek out the person who was interrupted in the middle of making a point and ask them to finish sharing. At a party, when someone joins in the celebration with a smile that seems forced, an HSP might look for an opportunity to serve as a listening ear.

Becoming an HSP Evangelist

The day I discovered that being an HSP is a thing, I became an HSP "evangelist." Along with the basics about what it means to be an HSP, I share these four assurances with every HSP God puts in my path:

1. **You're not to blame.** You didn't ask to be a Highly Sensitive Person. You didn't bring it upon yourself, nor are you making it up. It's not your fault; it is your responsibility.

2. **You're not alone.** You're in good company: 15-20 percent of all people are Highly Sensitive Persons. This means when you're in a group of 100, there are 15-20 others you can introduce yourself to and say, "Welcome to the normal minority!"

3. **It's not too late.** Many of us are finding out we're an HSP (how shall I phrase this?) "later in life." When I read emails from women in their 70s and 80s saying, "I feel understood for the first time in my entire life!" I weep for all their decades of feeling misunderstood. I am thrilled when women tell me, with glistening eyes, "I finally feel free to be who God created me to be!" Their joy is both encouraging and contagious.

> YOU CAN RELY ON JESUS,
> THE STRENGTH OF EVERY TENDER HEART, AND
> YOU CAN BE BOTH SENSITIVE AND STRONG.

4. **Yes, you can!** You can learn what it means to be an HSP. You can discover ways to maximize the upsides and minimize the downsides. You can rely on Jesus, the strength of every tender heart, and you can be both sensitive and strong.

3

The Five Fallacies of Sensitivity

Understanding What It Does
Not Mean to Be an HSP

Denise

After climbing a steep rock face, my toes crept toward the highest point of the cliff. I carefully peered over the edge to spy the rushing water below. From across the river, I had watched my two older brothers jump off this 20-foot cliff countless times. They would flip and twist midair until—at the last second—they would dive headfirst into the cold mountain water.

My oldest brother taunted, "You're not afraid, are you?"

"Of course not!" I retorted. But everything looked different from this vantage point. I wanted to get my bearings and map out my swim after I entered the water. Should I swim back to the other side of the river, which was a longer distance, or should I return to this side, which meant another cliff-jump? I decided to swim across because I didn't want to stand here again with a line of kids growing behind me.

Now I had to decide if I should jump, dive, or attempt a flip mid-flight.

"Come on! Hurry up!"

I didn't recognize the voice shouting at me, but I felt my body stiffen with the added pressure. I wanted to impress my brothers with a flip, but maybe I should practice with a jump first? Yes, a simple jump. That's what I would do.

With my plan in place, I stepped away from the ledge to give myself a running start, and with a deep breath, I flung my eight-year-old body over the edge of the cliff and into the water.

Down. Down. Down. The momentum carried me farther into the deep than I expected until my feet touched a sharp rock at the bottom, so I kicked as hard as I could to fight my way back to the surface. Once I could breathe in oxygen again, I swam to the safety of the other shoreline where I could admire my brothers' bravado from a comfortable distance. I could say I had done it. And that was enough for me.

Nobody Was Gonna Call Me Weak or Scared

Being the only girl in a family with much older brothers meant I was dared to try things—like jumping off a cliff or chewing a chili pepper—just for the fun of it. My particular family dynamic meant that I learned to hang with the boys. My brothers were neighborhood legends, known for their daredevil stunts, like flipping out of swing sets and flying off rooftops. By contrast, I was quieter and far more cautious. For a long time, I thought it was because I was a girl and they were boys, but most of the neighborhood kids—girls included—followed right along with whatever madcap scheme my brothers hatched.

I was different. That much was obvious, but sometimes I pretended to be more adventurous than I wanted. Nobody was going to call me weak or scared or sensitive. And nobody would ever, under any circumstances, catch me crying—not this girl, not ever.

When I read about Sensory Processing Sensitivity (SPS) years later, I shook my head. I had to admit that I could relate to the concept of sensory overload. Strong perfume nauseated me. Constant noise flustered me. Tight clothing bothered me. Still, I wasn't about to call myself a Highly Sensitive Person. If my brothers or other family members caught whiff of it, I'd never hear the end of it. So, I chose to investigate it more, but quietly.

Over time, and with much research, I had to concede—I definitely experience SPS. It's like a backdrop to my everyday existence, but I struggle with the term "Highly Sensitive Person." The connotations are all wrong, and it's the last club I'd ever voluntarily join. So, when

Cheri approached me about the possibility of writing a book on the subject, I told her honestly, "I'm not the poster-girl for HSPs. I cannot overstate how much I dislike the label."

Cheri came right back and said, "I have a hunch there are a lot of HSPs out there who are like you. They don't want to be associated with the word *sensitive*, so they're still trying to be someone they're not."

That's what got me. I spent so many years trying to be the risk-taking, roller-coaster-loving, adventure-living kind of girl instead of the quiet girl who wanted to curl up under a soft blanket and read a book with a cup of tea. That girl sounded boring, and I desperately wanted not to be boring.

Maybe that's you, too. Maybe you've tried to fit in by doing all the things you thought you were supposed to do only to discover that it left you feeling drained. Maybe you loathe the idea of being labeled "sensitive" as much as I do, and you're hesitant to get on this HSP train. (Don't worry. It's a quiet train, and everyone is in their own compartment anyway.) If that's you, you're not alone. Together we can debunk some of the myths about being an HSP.

Five Fallacies of Being an HSP

Sometimes it helps to understand what something is by recognizing what it is not. The following are five fallacies of being an HSP.

Fallacy #1: HSPs are HIPs—Highly Inefficient Persons.

In many work settings, those who are decisive and quick to act are perceived as strong leaders. After all, action means movement, and movement in any direction is usually viewed as better than remaining idle and stagnant. Moreover, the people who seem to get a lot done in a short period of time are generally regarded as more proficient and more productive.

One of the primary characteristics of an HSP, however, is depth of processing.[1] HSPs need time to process information slowly. They're hesitant to make decisions until they've gathered all the facts and considered all the possible choices with their potential ramifications—like the eight-year-old me who wanted to take in my surroundings before leaping off a cliff. This slowness to process data leads some to believe HSPs are less efficient than their peers, who are swift to act and quick to make decisions. In reality, HSPs can contribute in ways that complement their coworkers. Where a non-HSP might rush too quickly, an HSP can pose questions for the team to consider before making a decision. In the long run, the greatest efficiency is made possible by drawing on the strengths of everyone present, including HSPs.

Fallacy #2: HSPs are HFPs—Highly Fragile Persons.

Of the five factors of sensitivity mentioned in chapter 2, I relate most to sensory overload. If I'm visiting a friend and a TV is on in the background, the ambient noise makes it hard for me to concentrate on the conversation. If I need to get some writing done, the last place I'll go is a coffee shop. The sounds and smells would be too distracting. If I'm driving my daughter's friend home and the friend is wearing strong perfume, I'll likely have a headache before I reach her house.

While an excessively stimulating environment does lead to sensory overload, I have learned to navigate the minefield of sensory stimuli that everyday life provides. Living with Sensory Processing Sensitivity does not mean I'm so fragile I have to cocoon myself in a cozy bubble. I can do pretty much anything anyone else can do, and I can function well in any given setting, even one that's less than optimal. I simply need to know how best to prepare. If an occasion requires a lot of time outdoors in direct sunlight, I know the kind of clothing to wear and I know to bring an umbrella (for the sun, not the rain).

There is no reason an HSP has to be a fragile snowflake, and there is no reason why others should have to go out of their way to accommodate HSPs either. The knowledge of which things affect you can equip you to be proactive in the face of overstimulating activities. In chapter 5, we'll discuss how certain stimuli can deplete HSPs while other stimuli can recharge HSPs.

Fallacy #3: HSPs are HEPs—Highly Emotional Persons.

The accepted belief that extreme emotionality is associated with sensitivity is one of my greatest peeves. Being highly sensitive is not the same thing as being highly emotional. It's true that an HSP and a non-HSP can experience the exact same situation with varying degrees of intensity. HSPs tend to feel things deeply, strongly, and personally. But it's important to distinguish between an inward emotion and an outward reaction. Strong outward expressions typically indicate that something is going on deep inside a person, and it's wise to pay attention to such outward expressions and discern the nature of their origin. At the same time, it's also possible for an HSP to feel something very intensely, yet not demonstrate a visible reaction.

> BEING HIGHLY SENSITIVE IS NOT THE SAME
> THING AS BEING HIGHLY EMOTIONAL.

For some HSPs, the strong feelings they experience may quickly bubble to the surface in tears, but tears are not the only means of manifesting intense feelings. We all have different ways of expressing our emotions. Not every HSP is easily given to tears. While sadness is oftentimes expressed in tears, which can be a natural, healthy, and healing process, some HSPs may be more likely to hold in their intense feelings. While some may be more prone to "exploding"—whether through tears or anger—others may be more prone to "imploding" under the intensity of what they're feeling.

All my life I've been more of an imploder. I tend to hold things in, no matter how difficult or intense. Unfortunately, this can lead to other self-destructive behavior if the response to imploding is to self-medicate with food or shopping or alcohol or drugs. For me, the process of writing has been a helpful means of getting my feelings out onto the page, where I can wrestle and reason with them.

Fallacy #4: HSPs are HCPs—Highly Codependent Persons.

Highly Sensitive Persons are known for their empathy, which can be a good thing. Highly empathetic people notice when someone in the room is feeling blue, and they can reach out in friendly, helpful ways. Empathy for another person's difficult situation might lead us to pray more fervently. Empathy for a family's hardship can move us to respond by meeting practical and tangible needs.

Empathy calls for compassion, and no one was better at loving others with compassion than Jesus. He is our example to follow. But there's a difference between healthy and unhealthy responses to deep-seated empathy. Empathetic responses are a natural part of living with a higher degree of sensitivity to the people in our surroundings, but that is not the same thing as codependency. As HSPs, we can choose whether our empathy will lead us to respond in a way that enables or a way that equips.

Fallacy #5: HSPs are HWPs—Highly Weary Persons.

HSPs are "noticers." We notice the steady hum of the dishwasher that most people don't hear. We notice the flickering light that's coming from the lamp in the corner. We notice the slightly grainy texture in the mashed potatoes. We notice when someone walks into a room with slumped shoulders. We notice the extra sparkle in a person's eyes that says he's about to burst with good news.

> NOTICING NUANCE IS ONE OF THE STRENGTHS OF BEING AN HSP.

HSPs notice the little things, the less-than-obvious things, the seemingly unimportant things. Noticing nuance is one of the strengths of being an HSP, but we notice so much we can grow tired from all the noticing. Being on high alert all the time taxes the brain. So, yes, HSPs do need down time. They do need ample rest. Some HSPs report needing more sleep than their non-HSP counterparts, but this doesn't mean HSPs are weary all the time. In chapter 13, we discuss the importance of including an intentional buffer of time as a proactive measure to guard against overtiredness.

Understanding the impact of sensory stimuli and the effects of an overstimulating environment has been key for me. At the end of the day, I have to say I'm an HSP, but I will forever advocate that HSPs should not be caricatured as highly inefficient, easily fragile, and overly emotional people who get sucked into other people's drama and then wear out from all the strain. That's not the story I want for my life, and that's probably not the story you want for your life either. We can tap into the unique strengths of HSPs and become people who are strong and who contribute in healthy ways to the people and the communities around us and the world at large.

4

The Way HSPs Are Wired

Exploring the Science Behind the Reality

Denise

My early days of wrestling with itchy Easter dresses soon gave way to adolescence and the desire to fit in. I wore what the other girls wore, even if it wasn't as comfortable as I would have preferred, and I acted the way the other girls acted, even if it meant being chatty and acting like I was having a good time in a noisy room full of people. I played the part. But it wore me out.

School days meant constant engagement. Sometimes I'd ask to go to the bathroom just so I could sit in a quiet stall for a few minutes to be by myself. Sometimes I told my friends I had to make up an assignment for a class just so I could be alone in the library while they ate lunch. Food wasn't allowed in the library, but I didn't care. Sometimes I needed peace and quiet more than I needed food.

Slumber parties were like a rite of passage, too. Anywhere from 5-15 girls would gather on sleeping bags in a living room to tell stories, play games, and, of course, stay up all night. Sometimes I watched from the sidelines, sometimes I joined the fray, but always I went home tired. I'm sure all the girls were tired from staying up too late, but I felt tired in a way I couldn't describe. After a party at a friend's house, I wanted to retreat to my own bedroom and stay there a long while. I never understood why I liked the comfort of my own bedroom so much. I worried

I was too selfish and not social enough. I wondered if something was wrong with me.

By the time I reached high school, my mom had gone back to work as a specialist in Human Resources. She became something of an expert in temperament analysis, and she loved everything about the Myers-Briggs assessments. I learned early on that I'm an introvert who recharges by spending time alone. This described me, but not completely. There was something more to my "special preferences" that the differences between extroversion and introversion couldn't explain. And again, I worried I was somehow deficient.

My family seemed to take pride in hiding emotion. We were rational, not emotional. We were strong, not weak. These are the dichotomies with which I grew up, so whenever something bothered me—a violent scene in a movie or a tragic story in the newspaper—I masked how it affected me. At the first sign of any sensitivity, my family members would tease me good-naturedly. They were never mean about it. That was "just how Denise is." But deep down, I believed I was somehow not quite up to snuff.

As I grew older I observed other people and noticed how most of them were less like me and more like the other members of my family. They enjoyed large gatherings where people told stories with lively gestures. They looked forward to loud and boisterous family games. And they were at ease in virtually any setting. But not me. I didn't know why I wasn't like other people. I just knew I was different.

I'm Not Alone and Neither Are You

I've since learned that it's not just me. There are others who process life a little differently than the rest, too. This became increasingly apparent to me as an English teacher, where my students would exhibit vastly different responses to the literature we read together.

Whenever I taught *Night* by Elie Wiesel, I was amazed by the variety of reactions. Elie Wiesel won the Pulitzer Prize for his memoir of his time in a Nazi concentration camp in Auschwitz, Germany. His firsthand account as a teen boy surviving three years of extreme hardship, including starvation and torture, is difficult to digest even for the stout of heart. But some students seemed to absorb the heartache more than others.

After reading a harrowing scene where a young boy is hanged and all the men are forced to walk past his small, dangling body while he still struggled to breathe, most students would cringe or gasp, but a few students would close the book and push it to the farthest edge of their desks, so visibly disturbed they couldn't read any more. Those same students would oftentimes come see me after class or during their lunch break and ask if they could read an alternative book. The descriptions of suffering stayed with them. They couldn't turn off the images in their minds, and the heaviness of the material lingered in their hearts.

The same book, however, didn't have the same effect on other students. As soon as the bell rang, the majority of students would blithely return to whatever conversation had begun before class—like an upcoming football game or a school dance. This isn't to say that most people are heartless; rather, some people have a more resilient way of absorbing difficult realities than others. This resilience is something I have envied at times in my non-HSP friends, and it was clearly evident in the majority of my students.

My observations led me to believe Sensory Processing Sensitivity is innate, even while recognizing that the old debate of nature versus nurture will persist long after I have breathed my last. But before I move forward with some of the genetic research behind this trait, I feel I should apologize to the HSPs reading the previous paragraphs. Some of you are still thinking about the boy in Auschwitz. I know. I get it. I'll tell you what I told my students who came to me and requested that I allow them to read a different book: "I understand that sometimes we encounter content—whether through books or movies or news stories—that is deeply disturbing. Evil exists in the world, and we shouldn't close our eyes to this reality. If something is truly gripping your heart and won't let go, perhaps it's because you have a heart that is best suited to responding with real empathy and care. Perhaps you are being prepared to serve people in the world who are hurting. World War II is over, but chaos and heartache continue on every continent."

I never let my students quit reading the book, but I encouraged them not to sit alone with such intense feelings. I encouraged them to share their feelings with a family member or perhaps write about their thoughts in a journal. We can do the same. We may be more sensitive to the material we read or the news stories we hear, but that doesn't mean we should sequester ourselves in a self-imposed bubble. Chapter 19 is devoted to this very topic—how to manage the minefield of disturbing stories and news, and how to respond to a hurting world.

The Innate Trait

As mentioned in the introduction, Jerome Kagan's work with infants demonstrates how different babies respond to the same stimuli in different ways. The majority are more relaxed and at ease when encountering sensory stimulation, whereas a minority of infants show visible signs of agitation. They flail their arms or wriggle about, and their discomfort is clearly evident.[1] At that age, though, this could hardly be learned behavior. To the contrary, this response mechanism is something with which they were born, and the effects of this inborn trait are being studied further today.

Since the 1980s, genetic research has resulted in DNA sequencing, but we've known about gene-differentiation since Gregor Mendel's peas in the 1850s.[2] As Mendel experimented with breeding and cross-breeding yellow and green peas, he discovered that each pea had what he called two factors. A factor could either be dominant (D) or recessive (R), so the possible combinations in any given pea were DD, DR, or RR. Each of the two "parent peas" could contribute only one factor to its offspring, resulting in recessive traits "disappearing" in one generation (if DR) and then "reappearing" in a second generation (if RR).

Today, those factors are called alleles, and an organism has two alleles for each gene, one from each parent. While several genes likely contribute to the responsiveness of a person's central nervous system, the genetic research on Sensory Processing Sensitivity has focused much of its attention on the 5-HTTLPR gene, known as the Serotonin Reuptake Transporter Promotor gene.[3] The alleles for the 5-HTTLPR gene are referred to as either long (L) or short (S), which leaves the three combinations as LL, LS, or SS. Studies have shown that people with the LL (long-long) allele are the least responsive to sensory stimuli and people with the SS (short-short) allele are the most responsive to sensory stimuli, and they comprise approximately 20% of the population.[4]

Our quiz in chapter 1, which looks at some of the effects that are associated with this gene, gives you a pretty solid idea if you're an HSP or not. But you can take a DNA test to determine if you have the SS (short-short) allele of the 5-HTTLPR gene. As of this printing, it costs around a hundred dollars.

The Potter and the Clay

Why are some people more sensitive than others? Most of the literature on Sensory Processing Sensitivity attempts to answer this question from an evolution-based worldview, surmising that it must be a survival strategy that has evolved in some homo sapiens over the eons. After all, HSPs are careful creatures, preferring to look before they leap. Those of us with a creation-based worldview, however, contend that science is not counter to Scripture. Science merely names and works to understand that which God has created. Our DNA spells out God's design for us as individuals.

> OUR DNA SPELLS OUT GOD'S DESIGN
> FOR US AS INDIVIDUALS.

Why did God design some people to be more sensitive than others? We could place this question alongside others like it. Why did God design some people tall and others short? Why did he want some people with curly hair and others with straight hair? Why did he give some people the ability to tan and others the ability to freckle?

The most obvious answer is that God loves diversity. Just look at the sheer number of different kinds of fish in the sea and birds in the air. The different sizes, shapes, and colors in the animal kingdom alone represent an astonishing variety. God delights in his diverse creation, and the same is true with the pinnacle of his creation—humanity, whom he created in his image (Genesis 1:26-27).

God created diversity because each person contributes something unique to the whole of humanity. Paul discusses this idea in his letter to the Corinthians, saying that God's people are like one body with many parts, and each is equally important.

> The eye cannot say to the hand, "I have no need of you," nor again the head to the feet, "I have no need of you," On the contrary, the parts of the body that seem to be weaker are indispensable (1 Corinthians 12:21-22 ESV).

Admittedly, Paul is not talking specifically about sensitivity; he is speaking more generally to the wisdom of a body of people valuing the individual members, no matter how small or insignificant or weak they may appear at first glance. Every person has something to offer, including the more sensitive members. This is part of God's good design.

> EVERY PERSON HAS SOMETHING TO OFFER, INCLUDING THE MORE SENSITIVE MEMBERS.

Nevertheless, I have said to God on more than one occasion, "Why did you make me this way?" Being the more sensitive member of a family or group is not especially fun. Sometimes I wish I could be less sensitive to things in my environment and more at ease with my surroundings. I wish I could be less sensitive to the words of others and just roll with whatever comes my way. I wish I could be less cautious and more of a free spirit. And yet, Scripture says, "We are the clay, you are the potter; we are all the work of your hand" (Isaiah 64:8).

If God made each of us a certain way, then it was for a reason. We can either focus on the disadvantages of being more sensitive than most, or we can focus on the strengths. In *Sensitive and Strong*, we choose to recognize the disadvantages while capitalizing on the strengths, which is what we dive into with the next chapter.

5

The Upside and the Downside
Identifying the Effects of Various Stimuli
Denise

The summer before I started high school, I attended a youth camp. On the first day, 200 teenagers gathered in a large meeting hall for some typical icebreakers. The camp leaders wanted us to mingle and get to know other kids, so they said to split up by grades with freshmen in one corner, sophomores in another corner, and so forth. We then had to introduce ourselves to the other kids in our corner by saying where we were from.

Next, they told us to split up according to our birthdays. If your birthday is between January and March, you went to this corner over here, and if your birthday is between April and June, you went to that corner over there, and on and on, until we were all neatly sorted into our respective corners with another get-to-know-you type of question.

Then, they said to split up according to our hair color: black, brown, blonde, and red. The two corners with black- and brown-haired people were packed. The third corner with blondes was full, but less so. And the fourth corner with redheads? I stood there with two other people, gawking at the 197 kids crammed into the other corners.

When you have red hair in America, you've known your whole life that your DNA makes you different on the outside. You're in a minority of sorts—a fact never more obvious to me than that day at summer camp—but what I didn't know was my DNA made me different on the inside, too. I was also in another "minority" that didn't have a name, and it would be years before I figured that out.

Finding "Your Tribe"

Perhaps like me and a lot of other HSPs, you spent your growing up years knowing you were different from most people around you, but you did not understand how or why. Then somewhere along life's path, maybe even while reading this book, you heard about SPS and a light bulb turned on, casting a new light on so many of your previous experiences. All of a sudden, so many moments in your personal history began to make sense and you learned you're not crazy. You're just different.

The Internet has been a key factor in HSPs discovering the reality of SPS. For instance, Elaine Aron wrote her landmark book *The Highly Sensitive Person* in 1996, but with the power of the Internet, a website on her book's findings is available to people all over the world.[1] More and more people have learned about SPS and realized they are not alone.

Today, many HSPs have found each other. With the ease of a few key strokes, the Internet has given individuals who span large geographical distances the ability to "find their people." In his insightful book *Tribes*, Seth Godin saw the immense potential of the Internet early on. He says, "Human beings can't help it: we need to belong. One of the most powerful of our survival mechanisms is to be a part of a tribe, to contribute to (and take from) a group of like-minded people."[2] This is especially true for those who have always felt like they were somehow different from everyone they knew.

Even though one in five people are HSPs, most HSPs try to hide their sensitivities. We may not know why certain things affect us differently than our peers; we just know we're not like "everybody else," so we mask our differences and try to fit in. Because of this, most HSPs grow up not knowing many other people, if any, who are like them. Like me standing in a lone corner with two other redheads in a room of 200 people, HSPs have experienced distinct moments when they stood off to the side—sometimes literally, sometimes figuratively—with a keen awareness that they're different. Thankfully, that's beginning to change. In terms of finding your tribe, Seth Godin says:

> Geography used to be important. A tribe might be every-
> one in a certain village, or it might be model-car enthu-
> siasts in Sacramento, or it might be the Democrats in
> Springfield. Corporations and other organizations have
> always created their own tribes around their offices or their
> markets—tribes of employees or customers or parishioners.
> Now, the Internet eliminates geography.[3]

For the first time in the history of humanity, people now have the means to find people outside their local area who share the same interests, the same hobbies, the same philosophies, and even the same genetic predispositions.

At the turn of the twenty-first century, online groups became a new way to gather with kindred spirits. C.S. Lewis once wrote:

> Friendship arises out of mere Companionship when two
> or more of the companions discover that they have in com-
> mon some insight or interest or even taste which the oth-
> ers do not share and which, till that moment, each believed
> to be his own unique treasure (or burden). The typical
> expression of opening Friendship would be something like,
> "What? You too? I thought I was the only one."[4]

It is fair to say that his quote has been confirmed with the start of every online group. The ability to find people who are "just like you" can be empowering and freeing. And HSPs have now found their tribe.

Taking a Good Thing Too Far

Since HSPs grew up in a culture that values outgoing, gregar-ious personalities, it can be comforting to find people online who understand your unique proclivities. In a few online circles, however, some friendly spaces have morphed into places where HSPs are not only welcomed, but also revered as people with "superpowers."[5] The pendulum has swung entirely in the other direction, making it fashionable to take on this new HSP awareness as the definitive source of one's identity.

For example, one online article written by an HSP states that HSPs can read people "like an open diary."[6] The writer says, "I don't read minds, but I know when I'm being lied to, or if someone pretends to be happy when they're not. I see past the masks people put on. I know their intentions, their hearts, their fears."[7] Another HSP writer in a separate article iterates the same idea, "You [as an HSP] can spot a fake from a mile away. It's pretty hard for a person to hide their true nature from you."[8] In other words, these assertions claim that HSPs make good lie-detectors. That's a pretty tall claim.

While it is well documented that HSPs are known for noticing nuances and sensing subtleties, none of the scientific research says we're fail-proof in interpreting all the data we absorb and process. Just because I notice a person's left eye twitching slightly doesn't mean I can readily detect if that person is lying. I cannot know—simply by looking at people—the intentions of their hearts. To say that HSPs are good lie-detectors is a bit much.

Another "superpower" that some HSPs claim to have is a special connection with animals. In one podcast episode by an HSP, the host explains how "HSPs can have deep connections to animals due to our empathy and ability to pick up on non-verbal signals."[9] I do believe I have a very special connection with my two adorable and amazing dogs. The problem, though, with this writer's assertion is that the non-HSPs in my family have a super close connection with our dogs as well, so I'm hesitant to claim this as an HSP superpower.

It is wonderful that we HSPs no longer think we're weird or unusual, but let's be careful not to swing too far in the opposite direction and think of ourselves as somehow supernaturally gifted by virtue of being an HSP, either. Like most things in life, being an HSP has its advantages and its disadvantages, and in this book we want to take a reasoned approach to these truths.

The Upside and the Downside

HSPs do have special strengths to offer, especially when they're allowed to flourish in the right settings, but they also tire more easily from processing everything they take in. Not all stimuli, however, are draining; certain stimuli recharge and refresh, and it's important for HSPs to know which stimuli have which effect. In the following section, we'll examine three areas of life: 1) our physical environments, 2) our social spheres, and 3) our internal states. We'll begin with stimuli that are known to drain our energy.

Stimuli That Drain

Our Physical Environments

Consider your five senses (sight, sound, smell, taste, touch) and all the sensory stimuli you take in, whether occasionally or every moment of every day:

- bright lights, strobe-lighting effects, 3-D movies
- loud noises, repetitive sounds, sirens, clashing background noise, ticking clocks
- strong odors, perfume, cologne, scented lotion, fragrant candles, certain oils
- unfamiliar tastes, new food textures
- scratchy fabrics, tags in clothes, seams in socks, hugs that are too tight
- constant motion from transportation

HSPs can handle one or two, or even a few, of these things at once. But too many at a given time and HSPs are going to feel depleted by their environment with so many physical distractions.

Our Social Spheres

Our physical environments are one thing, but as soon as people enter the scene and we need to engage with others, sensory stimuli increase dramatically. HSPs are particularly known to avoid:

- large crowds
- crowded restaurants and shopping centers
- places where the expectation is to interact with strangers
- conversations with people who are known to talk nonstop
- conversations with people who never move past small talk
- prolonged engagement, such as all-day seminars or week-end-long retreats

It's not exposure to individual people that is problematic, but rather the overwhelming excess of so many people in one place or an extended period of time during which you're expected to be "on" that is exhausting.

Our Internal States

In addition to everything happening in our external world, even more happens in our internal world. Mentally and emotionally, we have much to process, especially when exposed to the following experiences:

- receiving a deluge of incoming information
- being expected to make quick decisions
- being expected to multitask
- undergoing a sudden transition
- learning of a deeply painful situation
- receiving harsh criticism
- watching a portrayal of violence on a screen or in the news

Again, an HSP is adept at managing one or two or even a few things, but when various stimuli are stacked upon other layers of stimuli, most HSPs feel an intense strain when they try to process everything they're absorbing.

Stimuli That Refresh

> WHILE SOME STIMULI CAN BE DRAINING TO AN HSP,
> OTHER STIMULI RECHARGES US IN RESTORATIVE WAYS.

Our Physical Environments

While some stimuli can be quite draining to an HSP, other stimuli have the opposite effect, recharging us in restorative ways. The following things are known to refresh HSPs:

- soft lighting
- beauty in nature or art or décor
- clean and uncluttered spaces
- muted tones for walls and furniture
- quiet spaces
- soothing music
- fragrance-free environments
- familiar foods
- soft or smooth fabrics
- gentle touch and gentle hugs

An environment with even a few of the things mentioned here can make a huge difference in the life of an HSP. These stimuli not only prevent an HSP's energy level from being drained, such things can also recharge HSPs, making them come alive in vibrant ways and enabling them to present their best selves to the world.

Our Social Spheres

Contrary to conventional belief, HSPs are not antisocial. We love to be with people, just on a smaller, more intimate scale. If you place an HSP in a room with a few people and the following conditions, be prepared for a deeply moving, personal connection:

- time to warm up
- interaction with small groups
- one-on-one conversations
- breaks from interaction
- few surprises
- conversation starters of greater substance than the weather

> HSPs ARE NOT ANTISOCIAL. WE LOVE TO BE WITH PEOPLE, JUST ON A SMALLER, MORE INTIMATE SCALE.

Much to everyone's surprise, an HSP can blossom into a wonderfully social creature when given the right circumstances. In such settings, HSPs can bring the fullness of their empathy and care to everyone with whom they interact.

Our Internal States

While HSPs generally have lower thresholds for filtering a ton of information, an HSP can be incredibly productive, and at the risk of sounding too braggadocious, HSPs can turn their inward focus into deep reflections and helpful insights when the following conditions are in place:

- less input, such as checking email and other messages fewer times per day/week
- ample time to make important decisions
- one task at a time
- fewer unexpected transitions
- predictable routines
- fewer stories with "shock value"

When HSPs are allowed to tap into their inner resources, they can make beautiful contributions in whatever setting they find themselves in. This is an HSP's "superpower," so to speak.

When we are aware of which stimuli drain us and which stimuli refresh us, we are better equipped to engage with others and the world around us in loving and helpful ways.

6

The Potential Pitfall for HSPs
Recognizing Learned Helplessness
Cheri

Today is the day.

Ever since I learned that being an HSP is a thing, I've dreamed of creating an online community for HSP Christian women. A safe place for us to hang out, check in with each other, support one another, learn and grow together. I started a Facebook group, but with nobody other than me to run it, I hadn't allowed anyone but me to post. My years as a chat host and bulletin board leader for America OnLine had taught me that online conversations need moderators, so for months I prayed for a team of volunteer facilitators who would make it possible to lift the posting restrictions.

Today is the day.

Six women have responded to my request for volunteers. They've received training in online community building and responding to crisis situations. They're excited to serve, so using my cell phone, I shoot a quick video:

Hey Sensitive and Strong Sisters,

I am here to make an exciting announcement that I've been waiting a long time to make. I am about to change the settings on this group so that anybody who wants to can post or comment. And we can finally have a true community for Highly Sensitive Christian women just like the dream God placed on my heart several years ago. And the reason I'm going to be able to do this is because we have a growing team of facilitators who have stepped up to volunteer to help welcome and make sure everyone feels that they're in a safe, welcoming, understanding space. So, I'm going to stop this video and share their pictures and names, and then they are going to introduce themselves. You'll know who they are because they'll have a FB symbol identifying them as a moderator. Without further ado, let the conversations begin!

As I edit the video to include our facilitators' photos and names, I find and purchase a lovely, slightly haunting piano solo to play in the background. The finished video moves me to tears. *Today is the day that dozens of women will begin feeling understood and find camaraderie with other HSPs.* I post the video in the group and send an announcement to the Sensitive and Strong email list.

And do the conversations ever begin! As do the concerns. Almost immediately I notice posts that feel more like "dumping" than sharing. Questions that include too much information. A pervasive sense of neediness. An increasing level of hopelessness. At first, I dismiss these concerns, telling myself: *It's just me. I'm being too sensitive.* Then, I quit responding to anyone who leaves a negative comment, assuring myself: *If I ignore them, they'll get the hint.*

But over the next couple of months, our volunteer facilitators become increasingly worried and confused. They had envisioned supporting women in their spiritual growth, not wading through post after whiny post.

"This is just a phase the group is going through," I tell the facilitators. "The group is a playground for our members to explore in their own ways. We are here to make sure everyone plays nice and stays safe. Our goal is to intervene as infrequently as possible. We want to reinforce conversations and comments that follow group guidelines and ignore those that are on the edge, letting them naturally fall into oblivion."

Then come the thinly-veiled suicide threats. We respond promptly and compassionately, reaching out to each woman with resources and following all the proper protocols for documenting and deleting their posts.

I begin receiving emails of concern from group members, like this one:

> ✉ **Dear Cheri,**
>
> I'm writing this because I joined your Facebook group for HSP Christians. I really appreciate the concept. Feeling empathy with others and understood is important. In all truth though, I've hardly gone on there because it seemed as though many people were looking for excuses to continue with problems instead of trying to address those things and give them to God.

Another email is more blunt:

> ✉ **Dear Cheri,**
>
> As an HSP, I have enough crises in my own life. I can't afford to be dragged into the crises of 1,000 other HSPs!

Group growth turns stagnant. Every time we gain new members, we lose just as many, if not more. Three months after removing administrative controls, I turn them back on and publish revised posting guidelines:

> All posts submitted by group members will remain pending until reviewed by the Sensitive and Strong facilitator team, which curates the content and timing of group posts. Currently, we are approving one group member post per day. We encourage submission of posts that:

1. Ask a generous question—one that is broad enough to resonate with many in the group.
2. Share a positive lesson drawn from Bible study, life experience, or a mentor.
3. Make a "Here's what's working for me" contribution.
4. Bring up an area of struggle, with a strong focus on problem-solving.
5. Invite concrete information, ideas, help, and support.

6. Aim to create a sense of hope-full connection among group members.

7. Promote a mindset of growth.

8. Direct our focus on Jesus as the strength of every tender heart.

Of the next 30 posts submitted, only five can be approved. Engagement dwindles. Six months after declaring, "Let the conversations begin!" I recognize that it's time to shut down the group altogether.

Lessons Learned

True to my HSP nature, I wondered: *What did I do wrong?* As I processed my disappointment through prayer, a light bulb went on: When I started the Sensitive and Strong Sisters Facebook group, I made two erroneous assumptions.

1. I assumed everyone joining would be proactive, eager to learn, and ready to make progress.

2. I assumed that once an HSP is in a community of HSPs, we would naturally, automatically bring out the best in each other.

The Great Facebook Group Failure taught me two vital lessons:

1. We're all at different places on the continuum of "Healthy HSP" to "Unhealthy HSP."

2. When HSPs gather, the path of least resistance leads to commiseration.

> WE'RE ALL AT DIFFERENT PLACES ON THE CONTINUUM OF "HEALTHY HSP" TO "UNHEALTHY HSP."

Turns out, there's a scientific term for the kind of commiseration that caused such concern in the group: *co-brooding.* Co-brooding is a passive "tendency to catastrophize and linger on negative feelings...when faced with a problem." Research shows that although co-brooding can make us feel bonded to those we co-brood with, it also tends to make us feel depressed.[1]

Parking in the Pain

"Do HSPs tend to park in their pain?" a non-HSP friend asked me.

I winced, wanting to say "no," knowing "yes" to be accurate but incomplete. Later, I asked an HSP friend, who happens to be a psychologist, "Do we HSPs tend to park in our pain? You know—stuffing our feelings so deep that we never process our problems. Or the flip side: rehearsing our woes to anyone who will listen, while wondering why we stay so stuck?"

"I don't think we mean to park in our pain," she answered. "Rather, it just doesn't occur to us that we can get out of the pain."

Her reply helped me understand what went wrong with the Facebook group. I had nurtured an alluring belief: *Wouldn't it be wonderful to live in a world full of just HSPs?* And I wasn't alone. New members frequently gushed, "It's such a relief to be surrounded by people who understand me!" I used to consider this high praise for our group. Now, I see the dangerous little word lurking within that positive sentiment: "relief."

Relief is a tricky emotion. It can fool us into believing we've made progress when, in fact, we just feel less pain in the moment. Over time, we can get hooked on numbing, escaping, or surviving the pain rather than doing the hard work of actual change. Since many HSPs have been the target of either explicit or implicit criticism from early childhood (e.g. *Why can't you be like everyone else?*), we are prone to get stuck in a narrow way of thinking known as *learned helplessness*.

Learned Helplessness

I first encountered the term *learned helplessness* while reading Dr. Henry Cloud's book *Boundaries for Leaders*.[2] As I read, I came to understand that learned helplessness is a passivity produced by repeated powerlessness. For example:

- The student who tries her best, only to receive a low grade. Concluding that she's too stupid to learn, she quits trying at all.

- The piano student who memorizes her music and practices her pieces to perfection at home. But during recitals, she is paralyzed by stage fright; each time worse than the one before. Seeing herself as doomed by performance anxiety, she quits taking lessons altogether.

- The woman who starts a healthy eating plan along with a group of friends for accountability. When everyone else shares their success stories, she feels so ashamed of her lack of discipline that she drops out of the group and goes back to her old eating habits.

HSPs tend to exhibit more learned helplessness from an earlier age than non-HSPs because we are so conditioned to question and even reject our own sense of reality.

Shifting from Temporary Relief to Long-Term Change

If you learned how to advocate for yourself during your formative years, you may have a strong collection of proactive strategies for avoiding, or at least recovering from, learned helplessness. But some of us have no clue how to advocate for ourselves because we never learned self-advocacy was an option. In fact, in many homes, it was considered disrespectful, disobedient, and downright selfish.

Our early inability to advocate for ourselves sets us up for the habit of seeking temporary relief instead of engaging in long-term change. This can lead to a host of unhealthy behaviors, such as:

- attention-seeking
- clinginess
- imagining the worst possible scenarios
- taking things too personally
- overreacting to situations

- refusing to seek help in a timely manner or from those who can give it
- requiring repeated rescue
- addictions to substances, experiences, things, or relationships
- perfectionism
- people-pleasing
- emotional meltdowns
- lack of boundaries
- masking over-sharing by labeling it *authentic* and *vulnerable*
- being overwhelmed to the point of emotional paralysis or "shutting down"

I hesitated to share this list, because it's so easy to skim a list like this and think, "That's me. Woe is me!" In fact, my purpose is the exact opposite.

HSPs DON'T HAVE TO STAY PARKED IN THEIR PAIN.

I want to assure you that not one of these unhealthy behaviors is an inevitable consequence of being a Highly Sensitive Person. We don't have to stay parked in our pain. We can get out. And the next chapters are devoted to exploring heathy ways to do just that.

The Difference Between Healthy and Unhealthy HSPs
Cultivating a Growth Mindset

Cheri

It's 11:30 p.m. as I tiptoe through the front door. It's way past this early bird's bedtime, but tonight has been well worth a few hours of missed sleep. Dinner with girlfriends at a favorite Mediterranean restaurant was followed by a live performance of Shakespeare's *Much Ado About Nothing* at a local outdoor theater set among majestic California redwood trees.

I haven't had this much fun in...yeah, I can't remember when!

I smile, sigh, start to unpack my purse, then frown. My gloves and hat, which were at the top of my purse all evening, have vanished. Digging through my purse produces nothing. Turning it upside down and shaking its contents unceremoniously onto the kitchen counter, I still come up empty-handed.

It looks like I've lost more than a few hours of sleep. And oh, how I hate losing things. My chest tightens as I do the mental math. My lost accessories are worth as much as dinner and the play tickets combined, doubling the cost of the evening. Self-recriminating thoughts begin to swirl: *I shouldn't have...I always...I'm such a...*

But even as old habits of learned helplessness try to hijack my thoughts, I hold them at bay with a vital question: *How can I be a healthy HSP?*

What It Means to Be a Healthy HSP

A healthy HSP knows herself.[1] She gains knowledge, strategizes in advance, and puts a game plan in place. My family calls this kind of proactive, personal agency "carrying your own jam jar." Years ago, we went on vacation with my brother's family. His son invited his friend Bobby, who was nine years old at the time, to come along. Bobby had a severe peanut allergy. He was so sensitive to peanuts that the slightest morsel could kill him.

Having never spent time with someone with a serious food allergy, I was fascinated by this young boy's knowledge of his own condition, the advanced strategizing he and his family had obviously done, and the game plan they'd put in place.

- Bobby brought his own jar of jam that sported a bright neon label with a skull and crossbones, plus the words, "Bobby's jam. NOBODY USE ON THREAT OF DEATH!"

- Bobby washed everything before using it. Silverware from the drawer, plates from the cupboard, cups from the drying rack—he washed it all.

- Bobby had emergency medication with him, a portion of which was doled out to each of us whenever we left the house on the off chance we might be alone with Bobby when an allergy attack occurred.

- Clear directions and maps to the nearest hospital emergency room were placed in every vehicle.

Like Bobby, a healthy HSP is able to take intentional, proactive steps on her own behalf because she's working from what researcher Dr. Carol Dweck calls a *growth mindset.*

Growth Mindset vs. Fixed Mindset

Dr. Dweck defines a growth mindset as "the belief that your basic qualities are things you can cultivate through your efforts. Although people may differ in every which way—in their initial talents and aptitudes, interests, or temperaments—everyone can change and grow through application and experience."[2] Living from a growth mindset, you have resilience—you take challenges in stride and bounce back from setbacks. And when you believe in Christ, you have more than just a human growth mindset; you have the ability to change because you have the power of the Holy Spirit living inside you.

The internal dialogue of an HSP with a growth mindset might sound like:

- My abilities are growing and developing.
- My efforts are worthwhile.
- I invite input from people I trust.
- I feel inspired by other women's successes.
- I'll try a different strategy.
- This is going to require my time and effort.
- I am being renewed as God transforms my mind.
- My mistakes mean that I'm learning.

In contrast to a growth mindset, a *fixed mindset* is a belief that "your qualities are fixed in stone…You have only a certain amount of intelligence, a certain personality, a certain moral character."[3] When you live from a fixed mindset, you lack resiliency. You're like a rubber band that gets stretched out but can't snap back into shape.

If a fixed mindset reminds you of learned helplessness, you're not imagining things: Children who learn helplessness early in life often become adults who live from a fixed mindset.

The internal dialogue of an HSP with a fixed mindset might sound like this:

- My abilities are predetermined.
- My efforts are wasted.
- All non-positive feedback is automatically criticism.
- Other women's successes are a threat to me.

- I give up.
- This is too hard for me.
- It's not worth even trying to pray.
- My failures define me.

How to Assess Your Health As an HSP

While external behaviors differ from person to person, the key difference between being an unhealthy HSP and a healthy HSP boils down to this:

- An unhealthy HSP stays stuck in learned helplessness and makes decisions from a fixed mindset.
- A healthy HSP intentionally moves away from learned helplessness and makes choices from a growth mindset.

> A HEALTHY HSP INTENTIONALLY MOVES AWAY FROM LEARNED HELPLESSNESS AND MAKES CHOICES FROM A GROWTH MINDSET.

How do these key differences play out in everyday life? Here are what a few of the differences look like in my life:

UNHEALTHY HSP	HEALTHY HSP
I rely too heavily on social media or virtual reality for a sense of community, becoming increasingly isolated.	I cultivate a real-life friend network to connect with and turn to.
I expect friends and even strangers to give me mental health support.	I consult with trained professionals and support groups to address my mental health concerns.
I use the phrase "I'm an HSP" as an excuse.	I refuse to use "I'm an HSP" as a license for bad behavior.

I confuse vulnerability with verbal vomit.	I am careful not to overshare and remember that "raw" is not the same as "real."
I look to myself as the source of change.	I look to Christ as the source of change.
I beat myself up for making mistakes, often for days on end.	I learn from my mistakes and move on.

To fill out your own "Unhealthy HSP vs. Healthy HSP" chart, download and print a blank version at www.SensitiveAndStrongBook.com.

One Small Step That Makes a Big Difference

To help me remember the differences between Unhealthy HSP mode and Healthy HSP mode—and intentionally switch from the former to the latter—I created simple diagrams of how we experience each one.[4]

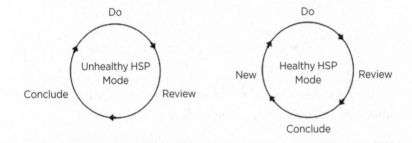

When you're in Unhealthy HSP Mode, it goes like this:

1. DO — You have an experience.

2. REVIEW — You ruminate over the consequences of the experience.

3. CONCLUDE — You label yourself and/or others.

For example, had I gone into Unhealthy HSP Mode the night I lost my hat, gloves, and earmuffs, it would have looked and sounded a lot like this:

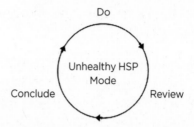

1. DO — My experience was stuffing my gloves and hat in my purse and taking them to the play, where I failed to notice when they fell out somewhere along the way.

2. REVIEW — My ruminations might have included thoughts like:

    - *I need to buy replacements.*
    - *But they are going to cost too much.*
    - *That's unacceptable.*
    - *I'll just make it through the winter without a cap, gloves, or earmuffs.*
    - *But then I'll be cold, and taking a walk with my husband will be miserable.*
    - *That's unacceptable.*
    - *I should call to see if anyone turned them in.*
    - *But even if someone did, I'm too busy to go back and get them.*
    - *That's unacceptable.*
    - *I need to buy...*

3. CONCLUDE — I might have labeled myself like this:

    - *You are so irresponsible! As far back as kindergarten, your report cards said, "Cheri needs to take better responsibility for her personal belongings." You are a literal loser.*
    - *You are a burden to your family. You're spending money on*

yourself that should be spent on groceries to feed your children. That's selfish.

If I'd gone into Unhealthy HSP Mode that night, I would have gotten stuck in learned helplessness, made decisions with a fixed mindset, and ridden the not-so-merry-go-round of rumination, perhaps for days. I might have posted a sympathy-seeking status update on social media, feeling temporary relief while reading the "You poor thing!" and "Oh, I hate it when that happens!" comments.

Healthy HSP Mode, on the other hand, looks and sounds like this:

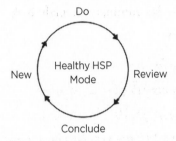

1. DO—You have an experience.

2. REVIEW—You reflect on your experience.

3. CONCLUDE—You learn from your experience.

4. NEW—You take new action(s) based on what you learned.

On girls' night out, I ask the key question, *How can I be a healthy HSP?*, and here's what happens as a result:

1. DO—My experience is still stuffing my gloves and hat in my purse and taking them to the play, where I fail to notice when they fall out somewhere along the way.

2. REVIEW—I remember that my girlfriends had kept shoving my gloves and earmuffs back into my purse all evening.

3. CONCLUDE—I learn that my purse is too small for everything I needed to take with me that night. And my careless cramming comes with a hefty price tag.

4. NEW—I decide to develop a new habit: zipping my purse all the way shut before leaving the car. If it's too full to zip, it's too full to leave the car. I either need to repack my purse, or I need to toss my purse in my backpack, which is larger, and carry my backpack.

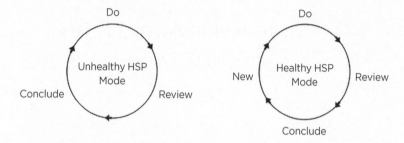

The difference between Unhealthy HSP Mode and Healthy HSP Mode is one seemingly small step, but it's the one step that will move us out of learned helplessness and into resilience: "New."

When we skip "New," we get stuck in rumination. In hindsight, I see that's what went wrong with the Facebook group discussions that devolved into commiseration. They went around in circles, offering temporary relief but no long-term change.

> OUR CREATOR SPECIALIZES
> IN MAKING ALL THINGS NEW.

Fortunately, we don't have to somehow guess or cobble together the "New" step all by ourselves. Our Creator specializes in making all things new. He promises, "I will give you a new heart and put a new spirit in you; I will remove from you your heart of stone and give you a heart of flesh" (Ezekiel 36:26)—which sounds a lot like exchanging a fixed mindset for a growth mindset. We're going to spend Part Two exploring what this can look like in the everyday life of a Highly Sensitive Person.

The Good News About HSPs
Choosing to Thrive
Cheri

I'm sitting in eighth grade English class, praying for a miracle.

For once—just this once—could I be more like Lisa?

Lisa and I are about to give speeches in front of the entire class. Once we're done, our classmates will vote to pick which one of us gets to speak for graduation.

As I rehearse my opening line in my head, Lisa chats nonchalantly with our teacher.

I want this so bad. But she's the one with stage presence.

Lisa is a born performer. Although she scribbled a few notes on a 3x5 card before walking into class today, normally she just wings it.

That would be impossible for me.

Such spontaneity is unfathomable. I've spent weeks writing and rewriting the three-page script that quivers in my hands.

Why can't I be more like Lisa?

The teacher calls my name. A wave of nausea washes over me as I walk to the podium. The next thing I know, my classmates are applauding politely while I head back to my seat. I have absolutely no recall of my speech; it's as if I gave it while asleep in a time warp.

Lisa leaps out of her chair and with one quip sets everyone laughing before she reaches the front of the room.

I could never do that.

Over the next ten minutes, Lisa effortlessly delivers such a fabulous message, even I end up voting for her. I don't begrudge her the victory; she deserves it.

But I still wish God had made me more like Lisa.

The Temptation to Compare

I recently read an article by researcher Thomas Boyce titled, "Are you an orchid or a dandelion?" In it, Boyce cites strong evidence that while most people are like hardy dandelions that flourish in many environments, we HSPs are more like delicate orchids. When conditions are harsh, we tend to wilt; when unattended by caring support, we can wither and fade.[1]

While reading what felt like my genetically predetermined future, I struggled not to feel discouraged, even hopeless.

> FOR ME TO COMPARE MYSELF TO NON-HSPs IS A
> LIGHTNING-FAST LEAP INTO LEARNED HELPLESSNESS.

It's a constant temptation to compare myself to non-HSPs, like Lisa in the eighth grade. Their lot in life looks so much easier than mine. Even though I've known I'm an HSP for many years, and I'm a die-hard HSP evangelist, I still finished Boyce's article wanting to whine, "I don't want to be a delicate orchid! Why can't I be a hardy dandelion?" But I held my tongue because I've learned how destructive comparison can be. For me to compare myself to non-HSPs is a lightning-fast leap into learned helplessness.

Learning to See the Sign

A while ago, I had an experience that taught me how easy it can be to overlook an obvious sign. I was driving through my hometown, heading to my parents' house, when flashing lights in my rearview mirror startled me. Normally, when I pull over and reach for my registration, I know exactly why I've been pulled over. But this time, I had no clue.

I rolled down my window, and the officer leaned down, temporarily blocking the blinding sun. "Ma'am, do you realize that you drove right through the stop sign at the last intersection?"

"Sir, that intersection has no stop sign," I said. Then we both turned to look. Lo and behold, a stop sign! A shiny *new* stop sign.

Mortified, I spluttered, "Officer, I learned to drive in this neighborhood. In the 30 years I've been driving this route, it's never been there. I didn't see it, even though it's standing there, plain as day."

The officer let me off with a chuckle and a warning, and now that I see the sign, I stop. I've switched from unconscious habit to intentional choice. It's a crucial change to make—in driving and in my life as an HSP. Where I used to automatically compare myself to non-HSPs—without even realizing it was happening—I've now come to recognize a flashing neon sign that signals, "Hey! You're comparing yourself to non-HSPs again!" And this telltale sign is either/or thinking.

Replacing Either/Or Thinking with Both/And

Either/or thinking is a basic survival mechanism that allows for quick decision-making. It allows our brains to cut through all the complicated data we encounter. In many situations, this is helpful. For example, when you're merging onto the freeway and a car in the right lane is traveling parallel to you, either you need to hit the gas or you need to let off the gas.

Either/or thinking becomes a serious problem, however, when complex situations are oversimplified into false dichotomies. A false dichotomy is an unnecessarily rigid polarization between two supposedly opposite extremes—such as, "Either you're a natural speaker like Lisa, or you're not." Other common examples of either/or thinking include:

- Either you're a thinker or a feeler.
- Either you're a leader or a follower.
- Either you're a giver or a taker.
- Either you're gifted with brains or you're gifted with brawn.

- Either you're more "right-brained" or you're more "left-brained."

And, of course...

- Either you're sensitive or you're strong.

This kind of binary thinking can artificially reduce a multifaceted complexity down to a simple light switch with only two settings: ON or OFF. These false dichotomies then reinforce a Fixed Mindset. Worst of all, false dichotomies confine human beings—made in the image of our infinitely complex Creator—to labels and little boxes.

For example, when taking the Myers-Briggs temperament indicator assessment, I come out a strong "F"—feeler. According to either/or thinking, I am just a feeler, not a thinker, which is a false dichotomy. On the Graduate Record Exam, I scored well in "Analytical Reasoning." Turns out, I am *both* a feeler *and* a thinker. The solution to the problem of false dichotomies is to replace either/or thinking with both/and thinking.

When it comes to understanding ourselves and other people, either/or thinking—like a simple on/off light switch—is an inadequate model. A far more apt metaphor is a sound board with hundreds of channels, each with its own slider. For instance, instead of being *either* a leader *or* a follower, you are on *both* the leader continuum *and* the follower continuum. The position of each slider may change as your circumstances change. When you're in a group with a strong leader, you may dial down your leadership and amp up your followership. When nobody else steps up to the plate, you may choose to do the opposite. As an HSP, you are like a custom-made sound board with a unique configuration of sliders on myriad channels, and your environment plays a key factor in determining where the "slider" will land at a given point in time.

Exchanging Comparison for Comfort

For simple situations and snap decisions, either/or comparisons can be a good choice. But when it comes to people, break down the word "compare" and the problem becomes evident: *com-* means "with" and *pare* means "equal." So when I compare, my goal is to make myself equal with others by making myself identical to them. Not only is this an impossible goal, it's an unworthy one. For in doing so, I—who am but clay—elevate my own judgment above that of my omniscient Potter.

When we succumb to either/or thinking, it is a sign that we need to stop comparing ourselves to non-HSPs and seek comfort from our Creator.

During a conversation with my wise HSP friend Michele Cushatt, she pointed out that the word *comfort* hasn't always meant "ease" the way we use it now. Prior to the seventeenth century, it meant "strengthen." As we discussed God's role in our life struggles, Michele reflected,

> So when God offers comfort...it's not so much that we are guaranteed the elimination of pain but he shores up the person in pain to be triumphant in [their struggle]. When God is comforting us, it's not physical ease...that he's promising to provide, but strength...in the middle of the struggle.[2]

God is constantly reaching out to us, offering his strength. Instead of comparing ourselves to non-HSPs, we can take comfort in him— the One who lovingly and intentionally designed us to be HSPs.

The Good News for HSPs

For all the seemingly unfair struggles we "orchids" face, there's a remarkable twist to being an HSP—what one researcher calls the HSP's "redemptive secret."[3] While we may be prone to wilt in challenging environments, HSPs are "more deeply affected by positive influences...more easily shaped by what is good and healthy" in our environments than non-HSPs.[4] Like orchids, we can "blossom beautifully" and "become creatures of rare beauty, complexity and elegance when met with compassion and kindness."[5] While we may have greater struggles than non-HSPs in certain environments, we can also experience greater successes, when the environment is more conducive.

I wilted on that disappointing day in English class. But over the years since, I've found learning environments where my speaking skills have been nurtured. I met Denise at one such conference. With time, my public speaking skills have flourished, and I now speak regularly for women's retreats and educational events. In fact, the three-page speech I didn't get to give at my eighth grade graduation became the foundation for a series of talks I gave in Serbia several years ago!

So, I've quit asking God to make me "more like Lisa"—or any other non-HSP. Instead of falling prey to comparison, I'm learning to pay attention to the impact of my environment.

The fact that our HSP successes are greatly increased when we are part of a positive environment is good news indeed. In Part 1, you've learned some strategies for adapting to your external environment, and in Part 2, you'll find more strategies for reframing your inner environment.

> YOUR MOST CRUCIAL ENVIRONMENT
> IS NEITHER EXTERNAL NOR INTERNAL:
> IT IS ETERNAL, FOR YOU ARE IN CHRIST.

But the best news is that your most crucial environment is neither external nor internal: It is eternal, for you are in Christ. We flourish, not as we focus on our struggles or compare ourselves to non-HSPs, but as we trust the One who is transforming us into the likeness of his Son.

Part Two

Looking Up

Let us run with perseverance
the race marked out for us, fixing our eyes on Jesus,
the pioneer and perfecter of faith.

Hebrews 12:1-2

The Trouble with Bubble Baths

Seeing Jesus as the
True Source of Strength

Denise

After a few clicks on my laptop, I let out a frustrated sigh. I had googled "HSP and self-care" and my screen immediately filled with countless articles on how to care for your highly sensitive self. I see titles such as "20 Self-Care Ideas for Highly Sensitive People," "6 Daily Self-Care Rituals for Highly Sensitive People," "43 Self-Care Practices for the Highly Sensitive Person," and so many more.[1] In online articles and other books, there's a strong emphasis between being an HSP and the need for self-care, and this close association has given me some concern. I'll explain what I mean by that, so hang in there with me.

As I said in chapter 3, I've been reticent about announcing to the world that Sensory Processing Sensitivity is a part of my everyday experience because the word "sensitive" connotes weakness and fragility, and that's not what being an HSP is about. But another reason I've been hesitant to get on the HSP-wagon is the prevailing connection between HSPs and the larger self-care movement. While I understand the need for basic self-care practices, I have some concerns about the self-care movement itself, as well as its overwhelming influence on certain kinds of HSP-thinking.

On the one hand, Scripture says the Holy Spirit resides inside followers of Christ (1 Corinthians 6:19-20). Our bodies are a temple of the Holy Spirit, so it's only right and good that we take proper care of our bodies. We need rest, nutrition, exercise, hygiene, and access to healthcare so we can be good stewards of the physical houses in which we live, move, and have our being. The Apostle Paul recognized this human fact when he said, "For no one ever hated his own flesh, but nourishes and cherishes it, just as Christ does the church, because we are members of his body" (Ephesians 5:29-30 ESV). In other words, it's natural to care for our human bodies, and God expects us to care for these vessels of flesh he has given us. Moreover, we can't fully live out our calling to love and serve others if we continuously neglect to care for our own bodies.

On the other hand, the self-care movement has transcended the realm of basic personal care and morphed into a ten-billion-dollar industry.[2] From expensive makeup products to extravagant spa treatments, self-care is a booming business. Luxury studios have sprouted in cities across the continent, offering a plethora of self-care options, including classes in mindfulness and meditation. Along with these classes, customers can purchase extras like vitamin-packed fruit smoothies or sea salt chocolate truffles.

In Toronto, Canada, the company Hoame offers meditation classes plus a sauna and salt cave—all in an effort to "combat the stress epidemic."[3] You can even book 30 minutes in their Dark Room. According to their website, the Dark Room is "designed to help you restore and relax. Each class is uniquely curated by our talented instructors who will guide you with their voice, soundtracks, and specially designed lighting themes. Hoame props, essential oils, premium elixir shots and cold/warm towels are included."[4]

I sure wouldn't mind spending 30 minutes in a darkened room, listening to soothing sounds with my feet wrapped in warm towels. But can everyone afford 30 minutes at the Hoame? Hoame is high-end self-care, and it represents the commercialization of luxurious self-care, specifically targeting the middle and upper classes.

Most self-care advice, though, can be reduced to simple practices, such as lighting a candle, sipping hot cocoa, taking a bath, reading a book, seeing a friend, taking an exercise class, hiring a babysitter, getting a massage, going out to eat, buying flowers, taking a walk, getting a haircut, or taking a nap. There's nothing wrong, of course, with any of these things, just as there's nothing wrong with a fruit smoothie or a chocolate truffle. The real problem lies within the subtle messages lurking beneath the behemoth of self-care advice.

Four Underlying Messages Within the Self-Care Movement

Steeped within the self-care movement are four underlying messages that pose a genuine concern. First, the self-care movement sends the message that you are the source of replenishment and restoration. In an excellent article on this topic, Christian writer Yana Conner makes a strong case for the danger inherent in this belief:

> If I'm the source of my own strength and I've got nothing to give, then I've got nothing to give. But, if God is the source and I've got nothing to give, then I can trust God will empower me to have something to give. And herein lies the danger of the self-care movement. You and your self-care disciplines can become your refuge and strength, instead of God.[5]

In other words, if self-care practices lead us to see ourselves as the source for replenishment and restoration, then we're displacing God as the sole giver of life and strength, joy and peace. That's not to say we can't enjoy warm baths or ice cream desserts or other simple pleasures; rather, these are gifts to be enjoyed more than practices to be followed.

Second, the self-care movement conflates necessity with indulgence. One HSP writer put it this way, "I'm beginning to realize that self-care is a necessity, not an indulgence."[6] In one sense, this writer is correct; some self-care is a necessity, like washing your hair and brushing your teeth. It's also a necessity to eat healthy meals and get enough rest. No one argues with the need for food, rest, and basic hygiene. The real problem is when self-indulgence is promoted as a necessity in the name of self-care—such as "eat chocolate (and don't feel guilty about it)" or "travel" because "one trip away could help change your outlook on life for the better and recharge your mental state."[7] These things can be a treat for sure, but they're hardly a necessity and not everyone can afford such trips.

It's true that HSPs take in a lot of information and can be easily overwhelmed, and it's important that we take care of ourselves. But we need to revisit what the real necessities are: Bible reading, prayer, time with friends and family, opportunities for service, nutrition, exercise, sleep, and more.

Third, the self-care movement focuses on your own personal happiness and well-being, not for the sakes of others, but for the sake of a happier self. One HSP blogger says it like this:

> If you find that you're feeling beat up emotionally…or feeling constantly anxious or sad, DO NOT berate yourself for needing to check out for a while to take care of yourself. Recharge. Talk to a professional counselor if you need to. Do the things that make you happy. Spend quality time with your loved ones. Do the things that bring you peace in some way.[8]

What's the underlying principle here? Do the things that make you happy. Do the things that bring you peace. Basically, do what you must to protect your energy stores and feel good. Yet, this is contrary to Scripture, where we're told to "look not only to [your] own interests, but also to the interests of others" (Philippians 2:4). Again, happiness and well-being are not counter to God's commands in Scripture, but they're not our reason for existing either. Our greatest joy is never found in serving ourselves, but in serving others, which brings us to the final concern.

Fourth, the self-care movement does not promote Christ-like self-denial or service to others. If we look to Scripture as the ultimate authority in our lives, then we will see plenty of examples where Jesus took time to be alone and pray. He took time to enjoy meals with his closest friends. In fact, Jesus spent 30 years in complete obscurity, all in preparation for his three-year ministry. So, yes, there is a time for taking care of certain needs before entering into service for others, but the way of Christ led to the cross.

The center of all of Christianity rests in the fact that Jesus gave his life so I could live (2 Corinthians 5:15). Jesus summed it up best when he said, "Greater love has no one than this: to lay down one's life for one's friends" (John 15:13). As followers of Christ, we are called to take up our cross and follow him (Matthew 16:24). This is contrary to everything the world tells us to do, and it's the opposite message the self-care movement tries to sell. But self-denial for the sake of serving others is the heart of every Christ follower. Not that we need to live a strict ascetic life without joy or pleasure of any kind, but that serving others brings a deep satisfaction that can't be found any other way.

Despite these four underlying messages within the self-care movement, the whole notion of "self-care" has taken root in our culture, even among Christian women, so it's clearly striking a chord with women and meeting a certain felt need. This is especially true among HSPs because we're accustomed to feeling overextended, and self-care seems like a good way to remedy that. But there is another way.

What Overextension Really Means

Many HSPs report feeling worn out from overextending themselves. Maybe it's because we're trying to "keep up with the Joneses" in terms of being outgoing with friends. Or maybe it's because we haven't honored the fact that we need downtime to process all the information and sensory stimuli we take in every day. After four and a half decades of living, I have learned this to be true: If I am desperate for some basic self-care practices, the reason is probably that I have neglected my human limits for too long. I have pushed myself beyond reason. I have stayed up too late for too many nights in a row. I have taken on too much, saying yes to more than I should. I have run myself ragged, until I'm barely holding it together.

When I'm spending myself in these unhealthy ways, there's usually an idol lurking in my heart. It could be the idol of productivity, in which my sense of purpose is tied to my work. Or it could be the idol of being needed, in which my sense of worth is tied to my relationships. Or it could be the idol of being admired, in which my sense of self is tied to my reputation. Or it could be something else. Nowadays, when I recognize that I'm pushing myself too hard, I see it as a refusal to acknowledge my God-designed limits as a human.

As fallen, sinful creatures, we continuously test our limits. Spend a few moments observing a toddler with a generous array of toys at his disposal, and what does the child prefer to investigate? Not the toys, but the limits. Inevitably, the toddler seeks to do what is beyond the bounds of his world. He tries to touch what he's been told not to touch. He tries to eat what he's been told not to eat.

We might smile at the cuteness of such toddler-like attempts, but we're not that much different; we just have more sophisticated ways of pushing our limits. We spend a little more on that outfit than perhaps we should. We add a little more to our plate than we need. We take in a little more caffeine to work even longer. I know I've been guilty of all of the above, but when we try to do more than what is humanly possible, which is another way of trying to be like God, we need to repent and acknowledge that we are not like God (Isaiah 30:15). We have limits, and we accept them.

God alone is limitless. In his omnipotence, he is all-powerful, requiring no sleep. In his omniscience, he is all-knowing, requiring no striving. He is infinite, immeasurable, and indescribable. He is God and I am not. This means I need to honor my human limits by embracing my need for rest, my need for balanced nutrition, my need for healthy relationships, and ultimately, my need for God.

I know what it's like to feel overextended, as many HSPs do, and I know what I need to do to take better care of myself. I need to take vitamins and eat more leafy greens. I need to follow-up with my medical appointments. I need to stick to a consistent bedtime as much as possible. I need to reduce, maybe even eliminate, my intake of caffeine. I need quiet respites periodically throughout the week, and daily when possible. But I don't see these things as self-care as much as I see them as humble stewardship, recognizing my limits and embracing them.

> OUR REASON FOR BEING HERE IS TO LOVE
> AND SERVE AND GIVE OUR LIVES AWAY.

When we are poor stewards of our health, we will eventually burn out and have little left to give. And our reason for being here is to love and serve and give our lives away, but we can't do that if we're constantly trying to do everything in our own power, trying to fill up with our own finite means of restoration.

Thankfully, God has a better way. Indeed, it's the only way.

The One True Way

We live in a world that worships shiny new objects. Whether it's the newest brand of sweet tea or the latest Apple product, we love new things. We get especially excited when a company comes out with a new way to lose weight or a new way to smooth away those laugh lines, but Scripture tells us something different. Scripture shows us a different way—the one true way. It's not new and shiny; rather, it's a well-worn path many have traveled, and it's the only way to life.

The way to finding true rest for our souls is not found in self-care, it's found in walking the path the Lord has laid for his people. This path isn't a hidden mystery either. It's spelled out in his Word, inviting anyone who comes to Christ to drink deeply from the well of life (John 7:37-39). All the self-care tips in the world cannot replace time in God's presence—reading his Word and praying. Jesus said, "I am the way, the truth, and the life. No one comes to the Father except through me" (John 14:6 NKJV). There's only one way, and his name is Jesus.

Besides caring for our God-given physical needs, the following are three things we can and must do to steward our bodies and souls wisely.

1. Be in God's Word regularly.

Instead of focusing on "good vibes," as some self-care experts advise, we can devote a part of each day to filling our minds with the truth of God's Word, which is living and active. The Word of God is powerful—powerful enough to transform our destructive thought patterns into life-giving truths. Instead of "thinking positive thoughts," which are fallible and prone to falsehood, we can set our minds, not on earthly things, but on things above, where Christ is seated at the right hand of God.[9]

2. Pray every day.

Christ made a way through the cross for us to enter his presence with boldness (Hebrews 4:16). Now, we can come to him with praise and thanksgiving, with supplication and intercession. Jesus said, "Come to me, all you who are weary and burdened, and I will give you rest" (Matthew 11:28). Rather than a costly avocado mask and a facial, we are invited to come to the feet of the only One who can provide true rest for a weary soul.

3. Observe the Sabbath.

Rest is such an important part of life that God didn't merely suggest it, he commanded it when he instituted the Sabbath (Exodus 20:8-11). The Sabbath is that important. There's nothing wrong with a bubble bath in and of itself, but maybe we'd feel less desperate for a bubble bath at the end of a long day if we embraced the weekly rhythms that God designed with his gift of the Sabbath.

> GOD KNOWS BETTER THAN ANYONE WHAT WILL TRULY FILL US, SATISFY US, AND MAKE US WHOLE.

To be in God's Word, to pray, and to observe the Sabbath are three foundational practices that lead us to understand our inherent limitations and our beautiful dependence on God. As our Creator, he knows us better than we know ourselves. He knows better than anyone what will truly fill us, satisfy us, and make us whole.

Pause and Look Up

When we're feeling overwhelmed and burdened, the most important thing any of us could ever do is pause, look up, and fix our eyes on

Jesus. Whereas most of the literature on being an HSP would tell you to put into practice a whole bunch of self-care tips, we want to encourage you to pause and look up, to keep your eyes fixed on Jesus. To this end, here is what you'll find in the rest of Part Two:

- In chapter 10, we'll discuss the ways HSPs can respond to stressful situations with confidence and calm.

- In chapter 11, we'll talk about why it's important for HSPs to find their voice and learn how to use it.

- In chapter 12, we'll help HSPs overcome those emotions that threaten to overwhelm us.

- In chapter 13, we'll look at the ways HSPs can work through criticism constructively.

- In chapter 14, we'll examine the importance of downtime and an HSP's need for a space of grace.

- In chapter 15, we'll explore the ebb and flow of community and solitude in the spiritual life of HSPs.

- In chapter 16, we'll consider the ways HSPs can embrace their empathy without buckling under the weight of it.

We understand that every person—and every HSP—is coming from a different place. Not every person has had the same access to education, much less the benefit of growing up in a strong, stable family system. For those who did not experience these blessings, they may look to self-care as a way of trying to "re-parent" themselves by incorporating some of the more basic acts of personal care and self-discipline that others might take for granted because such things were automatic in the home in which they were raised. We get it. We're not trying to minimize healthy disciplines, but the most important thing we could ever do is pause, look up, and fix our eyes on Christ, who is the true source of strength for tender hearts.

In his unrelenting grace toward us, God remembers that we are but dust. We are clay vessels, always in need of the Potter's hand to reshape us and mold us and guide us. We're so thankful that Christ is our Savior—we are not!—and we can look to him, who promises to provide for all our needs (Philippians 4:19).

10

The Struggle with Stressful Situations

Countering the Chaos with Confidence and Calm

Cheri

A child's panicked cries are quickly drowned out by laughter. The sudden shooting flames frighten him, and the adults around him are amused by his reaction.

I feel sorry for the kid. This is my first visit to a restaurant where food is prepared at the table, so I didn't expect a wall of fire to erupt either. But at least my first experience is watching it from across the room. For the child, it's happening inches from his face.

A few minutes later, another family with a small boy, maybe three or four years old, is seated at the table across from us. As the chef wheels his cart next to the grill, the boy studies his every move while I go into Personality Trainer mode: *Careful attention to detail, this one. Doesn't like surprises. Very sensitive to public embarrassment.*

I worry for the little guy. How will he react to the fire? Will his parents laugh if he cries? The chef juggles his knives, cracks eggs mid-air, and drizzles oil on the grill. With great mystery, he tells the boy, "Watch this!"

I watch the boy.

Through the flames, I see him do something he's probably done countless times already in his young life. It's an instinctive movement—so quick, I would have missed it if I hadn't been watching so intently.

He looks up.

Eyes wide, eyebrows up, he looks at his father, wordlessly asking: *Daddy, what does this mean? How should I feel? What should I do?*

The child's father meets his gaze with a warm, reassuring smile that says: *I'm here. You're not alone. We're in this together.*

At the next burst of flame, the boy flinches only slightly, keeping his eyes fixed on the culinary show before him. By the third explosion, he bursts out in delighted laughter. His father joins him.

On the drive home, I reflect on the split-second glance I witnessed between the child and his father. I wonder whether the father was aware of all he was doing in that brief moment: affirming, mentoring, bestowing a blessing. And then, in the quiet, I ask myself a far more personal question: *Where do I look when I feel overwhelmed?*

The Need for Space to Pause and Look Up

I long to be like that little boy. Don't you? I want my instinct to be, in any situation that overstimulates my HSP body and overwhelms my HSP heart, to look up to my Father. To do this, we must intentionally create a space to pause and look up in times of stress.

Psychologist Rollo May writes, "Freedom is the individual's capacity *to know that he is the determined one,* to pause between stimulus and response and thus to throw his weight, however slight it may be, on the side of one particular response among several possible ones."[1] When there's a space between stimulus and response, we have time to make an intentional, mature choice. However, when there's no space, we're far more likely to behave based on immature instinct.

I'll never forget the first time I recognized my own lack of space between stimulus and response. I was attending an intensive small group training for aspiring writers and speakers, where two well-known authors I greatly admired—Florence and Marita Littauer—served as our mentors. After giving my ten-minute speech, I sat and listened as Marita critiqued my presentation. Out of the blue, Florence said, "Cheri, stop interrupting! Quit being so defensive. She's here to help you." Startled, I replied, "I wasn't interrupting, I was just..." to which Florence responded, "You're doing it again! You've interrupted

Marita three separate times to explain yourself. You need to be quiet. Listen. And take notes."

This was a huge wake-up call for me. I'd been oblivious to what was obvious to everyone around me: the immaturity of my instinctive behaviors. I had no clue that I'd been interrupting; I thought I'd been listening. I felt not only momentarily embarrassed that day but also deeply convicted that I needed to turn this area of my life over to God for him to reshape. And I needed to start paying close attention to the all-important space between stimulus and response.

In this scenario, criticism was the stimulus; interrupting was my automatic response. We have a word for this kind of knee-jerk instinct, and I used to believe it was *emotion*. But it's not *emotion*—it's *reaction*. When there's too little space between stimulus and response, emotionality is not the problem—reactivity is.

What Happens When There's No Space

Years ago in science class, we learned that the primary stress reactions (also known as fear reactions, threat reactions, and anxiety reactions) are Fight and Flight.

Whatever you call them, Fight and Flight are the obvious—and infamous—twins of reactivity. They are opposites: Fight engages while Flight escapes. But they aren't the only siblings in the family. They're just the most outgoing. Fight and Flight have two siblings that are far more reticent: Freeze[2] and Fawn.[3]

Freeze stops you dead in your tracks, which isn't necessarily a bad thing. Pausing to assess a situation before reacting can be your wisest option. Freeze becomes a problem when, instead of intentionally choosing an active response, you continue to "play dead."

Fawn is stress or anxiety dressed up as extreme niceness. When you're mid-Fawn, you say things like, "Oh, it's no problem!" and "Of course, I understand!" Externally, Fawn may look like love, but internally, you feel the difference. Fawn is all about being conciliatory, no matter how many little white lies you have to tell. Love, by contrast, invites candor; love tells the truth and hears the truth.

The Problem with Pretending to Be Okay When You're Not

When overstimulated, HSPs tend to exhibit Freeze and Fawn behaviors. On the outside, we may appear calm and cooperative, but on the inside, our bodies and brains are flooded with adrenaline. This stress hormone can make our heart rates and breathing speed up, our hands and voices shake, and our ability to recall facts and string together coherent sentences utterly vanish.

When under the influence of such adrenaline, you may silently repeat a familiar HSP refrain, "Don't overreact...don't overreact...don't overreact."

And there's my go-to: "Don't cry...don't cry...don't cry." After all, I've spent my life hearing, "You're just too emotional!" from those in authority: parents, teachers, bosses. And when people say, "You're just too emotional!" with such confidence, it's easy to assume they're always right.

But what if they're not?

When someone asked Jesus, "What is the greatest of all the commandments?" he did not say, "Love the Lord your God with all your soul and with all your mind and with all your strength—but cut out your heart." Jesus actually said, "Love the Lord your God with all your heart and with all your soul and with all your mind and with all your strength" (Mark 12:30). Jesus calls us to live and love with our heart and soul and mind and strength completely integrated and intact.

> JESUS CALLS US TO LIVE AND LOVE
> WITH OUR HEART, SOUL, MIND AND STRENGTH
> COMPLETELY INTEGRATED AND INTACT.

What if we've named the problem wrong all along? What if our emotions aren't the enemy?

Learning to Grow the Gap

The solution to reactivity isn't suppressing, denying, or removing your emotions. It's learning how to grow the gap between stimulus and response, so that instead of reacting on instinct you respond with the power of choice. And the first step is what I watched the little boy in the restaurant do: Look up.

1. Look up.

When we look around—expecting fallible people to help us manage our immediate stress reactions—they often respond to us with skepticism and scorn. But not Jesus. Jesus's strongest reprimands were not directed at people for their instinctive reactions; they were usually directed at people's intentional thoughts and calculated actions. For example, while holding a child, Jesus said to the crowd of adults, "If anyone causes one of these little ones—those who believe in me—to stumble, it would be better for them to have a large millstone hung around their neck and to be drowned in the depths of the sea" (Matthew 18:6). In other words, it is the deliberate intent to cause someone to stumble that receives such a strong reprimand.

In another example, while clearing the temple courts of merchandise-sellers and money-changers, Jesus said, "Get these out of here! Stop turning my Father's house into a market!" (John 2:16) as he overturned tables. Again, Jesus's strongest reprimands were reserved for those who had defiled the temple with their deliberate actions.

On the other hand, when Jesus observed sincere emotion, he didn't call people on the carpet; instead, he brought them closer to him. One time a woman came to him weeping, and she poured an alabaster jar of perfume over his feet and washed them with her hair. Talk about a display of emotion! And what did Jesus do? He said to the snickering men in the room, "Leave her alone" (John 12:7).

> WHEN WE FIX OUR EYES ON CHRIST,
> WE'LL RECEIVE THE SAME REASSURANCE:
> *I'M HERE. YOU'RE NOT ALONE. WE'RE IN THIS TOGETHER.*

When the woman at his feet looked up at him, what did she see? Not scorn for her emotion. Not contempt for her devotion. She saw the purest compassion and grace she had ever known. That's how he sees you too.

When we look up, when we fix our eyes on Christ, we'll receive the same reassurance the father showed the little boy in the restaurant: *I'm here. You're not alone. We're in this together.*

Looking up expands the space between stimulus and response.

Then, after looking up, the following steps can help us dial down our reactivity during Freeze and Fawn reactions, thereby increasing our ability to make intentional, more mature choices.

2. Notice and name.

It used to be that when everyone stared at me in a restaurant, wondering why I was taking so long to place my order, I would think: *I feel so stupid. Why can't I make a decision faster?*

Now, I notice and name my behavior: *Hmmm. I went into a Freeze reaction.*

Before, when the waiter suggested the catch of the day, even though I don't like salmon, I'd say, "Sounds great! I'll take it!" Then I'd think: *I'm such a pushover! Why am I so spineless?*

Now, I notice and name: *Hmmm. I went into a Fawn reaction.* The "hmmm" part is vital. There's no judgment in this step. Just notice and name. This grows the gap between stimulus and response.

3. Normalize.

Remind yourself how certain reactions are normal for all humans and especially normal for you with a finely-tuned nervous system that's preset to high alert.

Here's how I normalize my own reactions: *I get it. I'm feeling over-stimulated because of all the sights, smells, and sounds. I felt like I had to hurry up and order, and I often cave under pressure. Okay, I see what's happening. I've never been to a restaurant like this before, and new experiences can be confusing. Once I'm more familiar with this place, I'll do just fine.*

Avoid comparing yourself to others or trying to make their normal your normal. Focus on what is normal for you.

4. Neutralize.

Some of us have decades of old negative mental tapes that play on autorepeat: *Why do I overreact to everything? Why do I take things so personally? Why am I so sensitive?*

Focusing on God's grace can help you neutralize these shaming inner voices, and meditating on God's Word will replace toxic words with eternal Truth.

Neutralizing my own negative inner chatter might sound something like this: *Emotional reactivity is part of my normal, but the fact that I sometimes Freeze and Fawn does not prove any of these shaming thoughts accurate. I will not spend my life trying to prove them wrong. I will invest my life proving God right for creating me the way he did—on purpose, for his purpose. I'm not the first person who has ever gotten overwhelmed by an unfamiliar menu at a new restaurant or said "yes" to what their server suggested. The next time I come, I'll have a much better idea of what I want.*

5. Make an intentional choice.

When you find yourself in a Freeze reaction, your goal is to get moving again. Some practical options might include: taking slow deep breaths, reciting Scripture silently or aloud, and prayerfully processing the situation.

When you find yourself in a Fawn reaction, your goal is to stop people-pleasing. Some action steps might include: requesting more time to decide, taking into account what you need and want, considering others' suggestions, and circling back to a previous conversation with more candor this time (perhaps even changing your mind).

You can find a printable version of this Grow the Gap Checklist at SensitiveAndStrongBook.com.

When You Feel Overwhelmed

Where do you look when you feel overwhelmed? When we look to the people around us to decipher a situation, we can get stuck in Freeze and Fawn, in a state of over-reactivity, with no space between stimulus and response. But when we are yoked with Christ, we follow His lead. He shows us, time and time again, how to look up to the Father until it becomes our new habitual response. Author and pastor Bill Gaultiere sums this up perfectly in an article on healthy relational boundaries:[4]

> Everyone is "yoked" to someone. We attach ourselves to certain people or things. We're prone to live with "insecure attachment," clinging to unhealthy relationships, staying in our heads to avoid emotions and intimacy, or escaping into addictions. Jesus shows us how to be securely attached to God and trustworthy people who give us empathy and grace.

For the rest of Part Two, we're going to examine different contexts in the life of a Highly Sensitive Person. Each chapter will equip you to create an intentional space in which you can pause and look up to your Father before responding to the situation. You'll sense his reassurance: *I'm here. You're not alone. We're in this together.*

And you'll respond in his strength.

11

The Problem with Pretending

Using Your Voice to Set Appropriate Boundaries

Cheri

Oh, but I know they love me!" Rachel assures me.

I've been trying to hide my growing dismay, but she can read me like a book. A high school senior in my girls' Bible study group, Rachel has just learned she's a Highly Sensitive Person. She scored 35 out of 40 on the "Am I a Highly Sensitive Person?" quiz. Many things in her life now make so much sense, both to her and to those of us who love her. But the story she's just told us about her summer leaves me speechless.

Rachel was a kitchen crew worker at a Christian summer camp. As soon as her coworkers discovered how "jumpy" she was, they made a point of dropping metal pans behind her, coming up and tapping her unexpectedly on the shoulder, and rushing at her face out of nowhere.

"They couldn't believe I still reacted as much at the end of the summer as I had at the beginning!" she told us with a giggle.

The "crowning glory" of all their teasing—and the reason my mouth is now agape—was to lure Rachel into a storage closet under false pretense, turn off the lights, and lock the door on her. When they finally turned the lights back on, someone dressed in a bear costume was standing right in front of her. As she screamed, they high-fived each other for such a stunning success.

My face must be registering abject horror, for Rachel reassures me, once again, "I know they love me."

Love? How was that love?

Rachel spent her summer coping with a body and brain unnecessarily flooded with the stress hormone adrenaline. In contrast, each time the others "teased" her, their brains received shots of pleasurable endorphins. It was more like bullying than love.

But the truly disconcerting part is that Rachel's two greatest emotional drives are for attention and approval. All the "pranks" played on her did, in fact, provide her with a great deal of attention. And as long as she engaged in Fawn behaviors—by smiling instead of complaining—she received a form of approval. So the vicious cycle continued, with a sensitive young woman using the name "love" for something far closer to bullying and a host of grown adults gaining pleasure from another's pain and calling it "fun."

The Uphill Battle

When I shared this story on Facebook, expecting my friends to share my outrage, I was stunned by their actual responses. The overwhelming consensus was that the pranksters had done Rachel a favor by helping her "toughen up" and prepare for "the real world." This made me realize what an uphill battle I had in front of me, trying to educate non-HSPs about both the scientific truth about Sensory Processing Sensitivity as well as the un-Christlike nature of the treatment Rachel experienced at summer camp.

In chapter 7, I shared the genesis of our family phrase "carry your own jam jar." At no point during our week together did we mock Bobby for his peanut allergy. We certainly didn't sneak peanuts into Bobby's food to help him "toughen up" and prepare for "the real world." We knew better. We knew that would harm him, not help him.

For a less extreme food example, consider cilantro. Some people find cilantro delicious, while to others, it tastes like soap. In our family, the split is 50/50: My daughter and I love it, while my husband and son grimace at the smell. So, when I make salsa, I put cilantro in half the batch and leave it out of the other half. It's a small but significant expression of love for my husband and son. I recognize their experience is different than mine in this area, and I demonstrate understanding and respect for that difference in the way I treat them. I would never force-feed cilantro to my husband and son, insisting, "Keep eating! Eventually, you'll learn to like it." I know better.

In many areas of life, our experience is vastly different than the experience of the non-HSPs around us. Some will understand and respect this fact; others will not.

When those around us understand, it's relatively easy to engage in conversations about our needs and preferences. Oftentimes they will initiate and welcome the information we share. My mother, for example, always asked dinner guests if they had any food allergies or preferences and did her best to accommodate them. Since most of her recipes began with a sautéed onion, she loved to gently chide my husband, Daniel, for not being an onion-eater. But without fail, she made onion-free portions just for him.

When those around us do not understand, it is tempting to stay silent. And yet, while the choice to keep quiet can feel safest in the moment, it comes with a long-term cost.

Learning to Look Up and Speak Up

I initially considered Rachel's story an example of the kind of under-the-radar, socially acceptable bullying that many HSPs experience every day. But the following definitions help me see how there was mutual culpability:

- When someone *unintentionally* says or does something hurtful, and they just do it once, that's rude.

- When someone *intentionally* says or does something hurtful, and they just do it once, that's mean.

- When someone *intentionally* says or does something hurtful, and they *keep on doing it*—even when they see that you are upset or you have asked them to stop—that's bullying.[1]

The phrases "even when they see you are upset" and "you have asked them to stop" assume that showing someone you're upset and asking them to stop what they're doing are things that healthy people do to set boundaries. Unfortunately, Rachel—like many HSPs—was used to "faking fine" by masking her distress, making light of the situation, or saying nothing at all.

This definition also forces me to face my own HSP passivity. For the first 45 years of my life, I rarely asked people for what I needed or wanted. I feared their reaction—or lack thereof—more than I valued my own integrity. One of the most valuable changes I've made since learning I'm an HSP has been intentionally finding and using my voice to set clear boundaries.

Here's one of my early HSP-aware attempts at using my voice:

A colleague used to think it was funny to sneak into my classroom as I sat at my desk, engrossed in grading while my class was taking a test. He'd tiptoe silently up behind me and yell, "Boo!" just to watch my reaction.

First, there was the seizure-like startle. Next, the jagged gasps for breath. Followed by the crescendo of ringing in my ears.

I'd whirl around to face the prankster who got his kicks from watching me jump out of my skin while my students stifled snickers. Knots would tighten in my stomach, my temples would pound, and my eyes would sting as I focused all my energy toward a single goal: *Don't cry. Hold it in. Don't embarrass yourself in front of the kids. Laugh it off. Don't make him feel bad. Whatever you do, don't cry.*

But one day, this prankster-bully sneaked up on me as I sat alone in my classroom. Even as my heart pounded in reaction to his out-of-the-blue "Boo!" I recognized what a rare opportunity this was. For the first time, he had pulled his prank when I didn't need to "fake fine" to keep up appearances for my students.

1. **I looked up.**
   God reassured me: *I'm here. You're not alone. We are in this together.*

2. **I noticed and named.**

Right now, I'm in freeze mode. If I do what I have always done, I'll fawn.

3. **I normalized.**

   I have always startled easily. This is normal for me.

4. **I neutralized.**

   I have nothing to be embarrassed of right now. If anyone should be ashamed, it's this grown adult who thinks scaring me is funny.

5. **I made an intentional choice.**

   I let my tears flow. I didn't lose control, but I did decide: *I'm not going to protect him from the consequences of his choices. I'm taking care of myself today. I'm saying "no" to an all-day stomach ache. I'm saying "no" to a headache that morphs into a migraine. I am telling the truth, regardless of how he responds.*

Then I stood up, turned toward him, and said what I'd never said before, "I don't like it when you do that." I swallowed, inhaled, and continued, "Don't ever do it again."

Boundary Setting FAQs for HSPs

For many HSPs, learning to speak up and set clear boundaries has not come naturally because we've spent our whole lives trying to blend in and act like everyone else. In order to learn a different way, we need to ask and answer certain questions.

1. How do I set strong boundaries without hurting people?

A primary reason HSPs struggle with setting boundaries is that we are hypervigilant about not hurting others, but allowing someone to feel pain isn't the same as hurting them. Had Rachel spoken up and said, "I don't like being startled. The next time someone sneaks up and scares me, I will report them to the kitchen manager," some of her fellow kitchen workers probably would have felt the sting of embarrassment, but Rachel would not have been responsible for hurting them. Their discomfort would have been a logical consequence of their own choices.

As you verbalize your boundaries and act on them, you can be careful and intentional with your words, your tone of voice, and your actions. But you cannot control how others interpret them or react to them. Use your God-given voice with confidence and candor. Then trust him to handle other people. Their reactions are not your responsibility.

2. Why should I speak up when I already know people are going to ignore me or shut me down?

I get it. So many things can go wrong when we set a boundary: People misunderstand, get mad, twist your words, start rumors, mock you to your face, mock you behind your back, label you, dismiss you, or ignore you. All of these are the exact opposite of what you are aiming for when you speak up. It's tempting to quietly decide, "I'll use my voice when I'm sure it's going to work. Otherwise, I'm staying silent."

> SETTING BOUNDARIES IS ALL ABOUT DECIDING
> BEFOREHAND WHAT YOU WILL DO .

Except here's the thing: Even the most well-articulated boundary cannot guarantee the results you are hoping for. That is why setting boundaries has nothing to do with predicting or controlling the behavior of other people. Instead, setting boundaries is all about deciding beforehand what you will do, communicating it in a clear and timely manner, and then following through.

Yes, the immediate consequences can be awkward, uncomfortable, or even painful. But with time and practice, you will start seeing long-term positive changes. You'll see changes in the way other people interact with you, but more importantly, you'll see changes in yourself. This is the most important reason to speak up, even when you already know some people are going to ignore you or shut you down: You speak up because you want to be the kind of person who speaks up—regardless of how others do or don't respond. And, every now and then, the people who you "know" are going to ignore you or shut you down will surprise you, and you'll be so glad you gave them the chance.

3. How can I set boundaries without feeling like an inconvenience to others?

Years ago, I was telling a counselor—in excruciating detail—how hard I was working to avoid inconveniencing anyone in my life. When she finally interrupted me to ask, "Why?" I had no response. I'd never thought to ask why! Then she said, "Inconvenience is normal."

Well, that was news for this HSP! Because of our perceptivity and our bad habit of Fawning, we are often adept at anticipating when someone might be inconvenienced, and we do our best to prevent it. While this seems generous, it can set you up for feeling like you've let people down when they experience the inevitable inconveniences of life.

> INCONVENIENCE IS NORMAL.

Trying to avoid ever being one of those "inevitable inconveniences" is not a worthy relational goal. Instead of fretting about what you do not want to be, focus on what you do want to be: honest, clear, and forthcoming. Sure, some people may get all bent out of shape when you speak up because your needs and wants may well inconvenience them in some way. As they huff and puff and roll their eyes, remind yourself: Inconvenience is normal.

4. How can I set boundaries with complainers?

I am all for having candid conversations and engaging in problem-solving, but I would rather hear nails screech on a chalkboard than hear someone complain. People's complaints can quickly accumulate to HSP-overstimulation, so it's easy to cave in to whiners. "What do you want? Here! Now be quiet!" Unfortunately, this typically creates a reinforcement error. They've learned that all they need to do to get what they want is to complain long enough or loud enough.

Instead of capitulating to belly-achers, we must develop a set of go-to responses. When my children were little, my response was, "Complaining kids are tired kids, and tired kids go to bed." When they heard me, they knew exactly what I would do if they kept complaining. Whenever a student tells me, "But Mrs. G., that's not fair!" my stock response is, "I believe the phrase you're searching for is, 'I'm so disappointed right now!'"

While you're building your list of complaint-responses, include yourself. I take the Complaint-Free Challenge every January, switching a bracelet from wrist to wrist each time I notice myself being unnecessarily negative with the goal of going 21 days in a row without complaining. Every time, I'm shocked to find out who the #1 complainer in my life actually is. Confessing my own tendency to complain is another opportunity to look up, create space, and pause before choosing my response.

5. How do I set boundaries with people who sound incredibly confident? Whatever I say seems so feeble in comparison!

Because of my HSP need for deep processing, I rarely make spontaneous absolute statements. I'm used to feeling and sounding tentative until I've had time to really think something through. Then—and only then—am I comfortable asserting a strong belief, opinion, or statement of fact. Not everyone works this way, though. It turns out, some people are very comfortable asserting many things loudly, without any research or reflection.

Years ago, because one student confidently declared a class project was "a complete waste of time and brain cells," I considered it a complete disaster. But when I compiled the class evaluations, I discovered everyone in the class except the lone dissenter gave the project high reviews. I almost axed the project from my future lesson plans, all because one student sounded so sure. Certainty is no guarantee of accuracy.

The more you speak up, the more confident you'll become. In fact, you might be surprised to learn how many people already think you sound sure of yourself. We HSPs can be our own worst critics!

My new hero is the child who sat behind our family when we saw the movie *Ralph Wrecks the Internet*. During the scene when Ralph is reading all the terrible things that Internet trolls are saying about him, this little tyke stood up in her seat and declared, "That's not very kind!"

I want to find and use my HSP voice like that, don't you? The more we look up, the more we will speak up with confidence, candor, and compassion—and take a strong stand for kindness, truth, and love.

12

The Turmoil in Tender Hearts
Responding to Criticism with a Teachable Spirit

Denise

I opened the envelope, having no idea what the words inside might be. I didn't even know who had sent the letter. Someone had hastily scratched my name in ink on the outside of the fold, and I found it lying in my inbox at work. I was 21 years old, and I worked as an after-school daycare attendant while taking college classes. I stood on the playground every afternoon, Monday through Friday, with a whistle around my neck in case someone tried to break the safety rules. You know, like trying to run up the slide instead of sliding down.

When I read the scribbled note, I discovered that a mom of one of the students was furious with me. Apparently, I had hurt her daughter's feelings the day prior, and the mom unleashed her fury on me.

Here's what happened. The school library was too small for all the kids to be inside at once, so there were designated times when students from each grade level could enter the library after school to check out a book. I was new to this job and still learning the kids' names, so some students would try to sneak into the library when it wasn't their turn by telling me they were older or younger than they really were. It was like a game, where some kids tried to see if they could get past me. I caught on to the game after the librarian kindly informed me that I had let some kids into the library when it wasn't their turn.

On the day in question, a small girl approached me and said she was in the fifth grade. The fifth graders were allowed in the library at that time, but she was so small I thought there was no way she could possibly be in the fifth grade. I thought she was trying to trick me like the other kids, so I told her she couldn't enter the library. Well, it turns out I was wrong. She really was a fifth grader, and I had hurt her feelings.

I found out about it the following day when I read her mother's letter telling me in no uncertain terms what a vile creature I was. After reading two handwritten, expletive-ridden pages, I sat in my living room, stunned. I felt awful that I had hurt the girl's feelings. I tried to imagine what it must be like to be so small compared to other kids your age. She must get teased about it all the time, and there I was, an adult with a whistle who didn't believe her.

At the same time, I also felt like I had been punched in the gut. The mom had been ruthless in her letter, and I was having a hard time digesting such mean-spirited words. All I could do was pray.

"Lord, I'm so sorry I didn't believe the girl. I feel terrible that I hurt her feelings. I'll apologize as soon as I get to work tomorrow, but honestly, I think the mom has overreacted here in a pretty extreme way. Please give me wisdom to know how I should respond to this letter. Help me sift through these words and hear what I need to hear, but also reject what I need to reject."

The Meat and the Bones

Criticism is a part of life. Sometimes it's well-earned and sometimes it's not. Whenever I receive hard feedback, I remember my grandma's words. She would say we need to swallow the meat and spit out the bones—a cliché, for sure, but true nonetheless. We should take to heart what is good and true (the meat) but discard the rest (the bones).

Whenever we're the recipient of harsh words, we need to filter the good—the parts that could help us—from the bad—the parts that are meant to hurt us. Of course, that's usually easier said than done.

For HSPs especially, filtering is taxing. Being an HSP is like being a colander with giant holes that lets everything through. We take in more stimuli (both physical and emotional) than most people, so we tend to take everything to heart. But this added measure of sensitivity does not mean HSPs should be spared from ever receiving criticism.

In an article on patheos.com, one Christian writer asserts that we live in an age of heightened sensitivity, and people today are less able to receive any kind of rebuke or warning. He quotes Proverbs 27:5-6, "Better is open rebuke than hidden love. Faithful are the wounds of a friend; profuse are the kisses of an enemy" (ESV). The writer goes on to make a case for why we need to be open not only to self-examination, but also to "the examination of others, particularly members of our local congregations."[1] The main thrust of the article is spot on. People should be open to receiving criticism, even hard words when necessary.

The only problem with the article is the opening paragraph. The writer begins by saying, "Are you a 'highly sensitive person'?" He then lists a couple of books on the subject, including Elaine Aron's, plus a link to a website saying these resources are "designed especially to assist you and, specifically, to lighten the heavy burden of your wallet."[2] The sarcastic tone conveys a disparaging view of HSPs, and he uses the new field of research on Sensory Processing Sensitivity as evidence that hypersensitivity is now prevalent in society. He says, "In a culture that values self-esteem and derides self-control and self-abasement, sensitivity is thoroughly in style. Hard words are out; soft words are in."[3]

He has a point, but he uses a straw man argument to make it.

This writer uses the most conventional connotation of the word "sensitive" to infer that HSPs are fragile persons who cannot handle hard feedback. But that's not what being an HSP is about, and it's exactly this kind of misunderstanding that makes HSPs like me want to conceal the reality of Sensory Processing Sensitivity. The truth is, while I do experience a heightened sense of processing stimuli on a near-constant basis, I am plenty capable of hearing hard words.

Strategies for Processing Criticism

Criticism is never fun. It means someone has given us a grade and it's not an A+. Receiving a poor evaluation can be painful, but it might be necessary. It's important for all people to develop the skills required to process criticism, including HSPs. The following are some strategies we can employ whenever we are the recipient of a rebuke. When we receive criticism, we need to hear it, evaluate it, and respond to it.

Hear the Criticism

Confrontation can happen directly or indirectly. If the confrontation happens directly, then either someone approaches you for a face-to-face conversation (which is always best), or someone confronts you in a group setting, which is not my recommendation as a first step. If the confrontation happens indirectly, then either someone approaches you through the medium of a letter, email, or private message (although face-to-face or a phone call is better), or someone criticizes you to others and you hear about it through the grapevine, which is the worst way to receive criticism.

The *way* someone comes to you with criticism makes a big difference. In a best-case scenario, the person who confronts you does so directly, face-to-face, but we cannot control how another person confronts us with criticism. We are only responsible for how we respond.

Whenever you receive criticism, first separate the criticism from the criticizer. In other words, consider the source. Does this person have authority to speak into your life? Is this person a spouse, parent, pastor, boss, mentor, or close friend? Has this person demonstrated in the past that he or she has good intentions toward you? Is this person well-respected in your circle of associates? If so, this is all the more reason to weigh this person's words. If, however, the criticism comes from someone you barely know and with whom you have little associ-ation, then the criticism takes a less important role. The information might still be good and worthwhile, but criticism from strangers gets a less prominent place in your heart. If the criticism comes from an anonymous source (and that's always possible in today's online world), dismiss it entirely. If someone wants to hide in anonymity, then their words have zero weight.

Once you've weighed the authority and influence this person has in your life, you will want to hear the criticism with an open mind, and the best way to hear it is to do the following:

- Say a quick prayer, asking God to help you hear the criti-cism with an open mind.
- Then listen to the criticism closely.
- Don't interrupt.
- Take some notes.
- Ask questions for clarification.
- Repeat what you have heard.
- Ask for examples. (Is this a one-time occurrence or a pat-tern you see in my life?)
- Invite ideas for solutions. This is critical. Don't skip this important step.
- Say thank you. Express appreciation, especially if this per-son came directly to you.
- Express your desire for some time to process what you have heard.
- Name a day and time you plan to follow-up on the matter once you've had a chance to digest everything.

Lastly, refuse the temptation to explain yourself or justify your actions. The person criticizing you has likely had some time to think about what they're saying. You are at a disadvantage because you have not had a chance to think through your response. And if you're an HSP, impromptu speaking isn't your strong suit anyway, so give yourself a chance to calmly sit down and evaluate everything you've heard.

Evaluate the Criticism

Once you've heard everything the person had to say, find a place where you can give yourself some space. Do not run to a friend to "download" what just happened. Do not jump onto social media and share your side of things. Give yourself permission to sit with the information awhile and do the following:

- Pause and look up by prayerfully seeking the Lord's guidance.
- Take note of your immediate physical state and take care of your physical needs.
- Sort the helpful from the hurtful.
- Consider the possibility that this is an opportunity for something beautiful and beneficial.

Let's unpack each of these a little further.

First, pause and look up. Prayerfully seek the Lord's guidance. Invite God into this area of your life. Ask him which part of the criticism you need to hear and which part you can set aside. Ask him to show you how best to respond to the criticism. Most importantly, ask him how you can show love, grace, and kindness to the person criticizing you.

Second, take note of your immediate physical state and take care of your physical needs. Are you hungry or tired? If so, it might be best to postpone evaluating the criticism until after you've had a good meal and maybe even a nap or a decent night's rest. Is your head pounding or your heart racing? You may want to go for a walk or engage in some sort of exercise. Do you feel like shouting or crying? You may want to spend a few moments writing in a journal everything you are feeling and thinking. Once you've cared for your physical needs, you will be better prepared to evaluate the criticism from a more objective perspective.

Third, sort the helpful from the hurtful. Did the criticism come with helpful ideas for solutions? If so, add to those solutions more of your own. Come up with your best proposal for resolving the matter. Did the criticism come with hurtful words about you personally? Was any name-calling involved? If so, set those hurtful words aside. Criticism involves something we said or did, so focus on the thing you said or did which prompted the criticism in the first place. Separate out any name-calling or personal attacks. Remember: Hurt people hurt people. If this person has come to you with criticism loaded with hurtful words, then it's possible those hurtful words reflect the person saying them more than they reflect you. Be like my grandma and swallow the meat but spit out the bones.

> YOU NEVER KNOW HOW GOD
> CAN USE A DIFFICULT CIRCUMSTANCE
> TO BRING ABOUT SOMETHING INCREDIBLE.

Fourth, consider the possibility that this is an opportunity for something else—perhaps even something beautiful and beneficial. Maybe there's something greater at stake than the thing you've been criticized for. Maybe this is an opportunity to build a stronger relationship with this person. Maybe your response to this situation will be a catalyst for something amazing in the future. You never know how God can use a difficult circumstance to bring about something incredible.

Respond to the Criticism

Okay, you've done the hard work of hearing and evaluating the criticism, now it's time to respond to it. But a word of caution first. Just as we cannot control the *way* someone criticized us, we cannot control the *way* the other person will receive our response. All we can do is our part, and our part is the following:

• Prayerfully decide how best to respond to the criticism.
• Prayerfully decide how best to respond to the criticizer.

- Carry out your plans.

First, prayerfully decide how best to respond to the criticism. Own what is yours to own. If there is a change you need to make, create an action plan for implementing that change. If there is something for which you need to apologize, determine the best time and place for making that apology. Then, make the apology, and make it in person. Face-to-face is always preferable.

Second, prayerfully decide how best to respond to the criticizer. Formulate a plan for how you will communicate your changes with the person who came to you with criticism. If you appreciated the *way* this person approached you, be sure to say so. If you didn't appreciate the *way* this person approached you, share the best way for you to receive criticism in the future.

Third, carry out your plans. That's it. At the risk of sounding like a Nike commercial, just do it.

Growing from the Hard Words We Receive

Being a Highly Sensitive Person does not mean we're incapable of hearing hard words or receiving criticism. We can hear it, evaluate it, and respond to it. Even better, we can grow from it. The day after I received that mom's awful letter, I went to work early and showed it to my supervisor. I was worried I might get fired, but mostly I was concerned I might have done irreparable damage to this young girl's heart.

My supervisor read the letter, let out an exaggerated huff, and with a wave of her hand dismissed the letter. She said, "Oh, honey, you're not the first person around here who's been on the receiving end of that woman's wrath. Be sure to apologize to the girl, and maybe from now on you can doublecheck with the librarian if you're not sure if a student is the right age to enter the library at the right time. But please don't take this woman's words to heart. She's the vile one." And with that, my supervisor moved on while I stood there with the letter still burning in my 21-year-old hands.

I found the girl and apologized. She accepted my apology and seemed a little sheepish, like maybe she was more embarrassed by her mother's behavior. Her mom had a reputation.

When the mom arrived later that day to pick up her daughter from school, I walked straight toward her so I could apologize to her as well. Just thinking about apologizing to someone who had been so mean was making my stomach turn to knots, but I planned to apologize for not believing her daughter and leave it at that. I would not accept the names she called me in her letter.

To my surprise, the mom avoided me. When I approached her directly, she turned away, clearly unwilling to have a face-to-face conversation. That's when I saw the cowardice in her behavior. She could be tough and mean when hiding behind her written words, but she was a coward in person.

In the end, I was grateful for the hard words I received, even though they were delivered in a mean-spirited and cowardly manner. I was grateful because the letter gave me the opportunity to pause and look up; the harsh criticism was a chance for me to go to God and learn how to sort the helpful from the hurtful. The letter became a way for me to develop some skills in how I can choose my response to criticism, even really hard words.

13

The Enigma of Emotions
Moving Forward When Blindsided by All the Feels
Cheri

This can't be happening. We arrived at the airport three hours ago: long before our flight was supposed to leave.

We did everything right. Yet here we stand, my husband Daniel and I, staring at each other in shock because our plane has just taken off without us.

We are stranded in Serbia. Our cell phones don't work internationally, so we can't call the event organizer who booked our plane tickets. We're on our own.

After receiving an hour of head shaking and *tsk-tsk-tsking* from an airline representative, plus paying a stunning sum of money for new tickets, we are rebooked to depart in 34 hours. What we'll do between now and then, we have no clue.

I'm a ticking time bomb of dismay and regret. Even as I swallow hard, my vision blurs and the fresh ink on the receipt in my hand begins to run.

This can't be happening.

Why the Emotional Dam Cracks

Now let's be clear: If another woman had missed her early morning flight, I'd be responding to her with instant empathy—even buying her a mocha and a blueberry scone. But when the mistake-maker is me, I have no such compassion. Instead, I snap into attack mode, with self-blaming and self-shaming-guns a-blazing: *You're such a screw-up. And a big baby.*

WE HSPs ARE SO HARD ON OURSELVES, AREN'T WE?

We HSPs are so hard on ourselves, aren't we?

Cognitively, I know that when I'm overstimulated, I'll probably experience *emotional flooding*—"a prominent, overwhelming emotion that creates a physiological arousal which activates and mobilizes the body to cope with situations perceived as dangerous."[1] I also know that overstimulation and emotional flooding can spiral into a vicious cycle of endless cause and effect.

The missed flight out of Serbia is the culmination of an intense five-day conference during which Daniel and I facilitated six workshops and copresented a plenary address. Now, I'm sleep-deprived. My blood sugar is free-falling. I'm stuck in an airport, an HSP minefield of sensory overload. And my internal monologue is stuck on: *This can't be happening. You're such a screw-up. And a big baby.*

You know from your own life experiences how overstimulation can trigger a tsunami wave of emotion suddenly bearing down on you. You know what it's like to be a grown woman on the verge of a meltdown. The moment you sense that a crying jag or angry blow-up is building, you need to create space, pause, and look up. Remember that God's presence brings us comfort, not condemnation. Recognize that your Father is with you in the midst of the turmoil, reassuring you: *I'm here. You're not alone. We're in this together.*

The Truth Behind "Too Emotional"

When a new subscriber signs up for the Sensitive and Strong email newsletter, she receives a welcome email inviting her to hit reply and share her biggest challenge as an HSP. Many responses pinpoint *emotions* as an area of struggle:

- "I feel too much."

- "My family says I'm too emotional."

- "Things hurt me deeply that don't seem to bother anyone else."

One woman wrote, "I've tried and tried to 'boss my feelings around' but it just makes things worse. What's wrong with me?"

(Note: These sentiments are not true of every HSP. If these comments don't resonate, you may be more like Denise, who says she tends to hold her feelings in and not show much outward reaction.)

While many Highly Sensitive Persons are used to being labeled "too emotional," a more accurate description is that HSPs tend to experience emotions more intensely than non-HSPs. While we all experience life more vividly during emotionally charged moments, this emotional "vividness" is stronger for some than others. As noted earlier, high sensitivity has been baked into our DNA.

The "emotional vividness" gene is related to norepinephrine, a neurotransmitter that also helps with the body's stress response.[2] One variant, which is common to HSPs, turns up the dial on emotional vividness. If you have it, you will perceive the emotional aspects of the world more vividly. You'll also have much more activity in the parts of the brain that create internal emotional responses to your experiences.

Most HSPs are keenly aware of experiencing inner emotions more intensely than non-HSPs. And we often pick up on emotional undercurrents where others notice nothing. If you're highly sensitive, this is not your imagination—you may actually have a brighter palette of emotional "colors," so to speak, because of this "emotional vividness" gene variant.[3]

Processing Our Emotions

In his reflective book, *The Listening Life: Embracing Attentiveness in a World of Distraction*, Adam McHugh suggests that instead of being self-critical about our emotions, we become curious about them. He says, "We ought to listen to our emotions before we start preaching to them. Let's not tell them what to do before they tell us what they are already doing." That day in the Belgrade airport, I used the five steps of the Grow the Gap Checklist to keep me curious.

1. **I looked up.** Instead of asking myself, "What's wrong with me?" I asked Jesus, "What's going on with me?" and listened.

2. **I noticed and named my emotions.** And their intensity. As the kind of gal who panics when she gets separated from her husband in Home Depot, I felt utterly devastated that our airline had abandoned us. I didn't behave badly or drag Daniel down with me. But as I entered into conversational prayer, I named my emotions: *I am experiencing shock, fury, and terror—all at the same time.*

> YOU WERE CREATED FOR HEAVEN, BUT
> YOUR CURRENT ADDRESS IS EARTH.

3. **I normalized what was happening in my idealistic heart.** My daddy told me growing up, "Sunshine, you were created for heaven, but your current address is earth." So yes, it's natural for my God-given idealistic heart to want the airline to find me rather than abandon me. And on this planet, it's also normal for things to go wrong. It's a painful paradox that comes part-and-parcel with dual citizenship.

4. **I neutralized the negative by focusing on the positive.** As we traipsed through the airport to pick up our luggage, I prayed aloud—"Thank you, Lord, that we have our suitcases! Jesus, thank you that we're in a safe location with a roof over our head during this trial!"—not because God needed to hear my words but because I did. Gratitude always helps me look up and recognize God's presence and provision in times of crisis.

5. **I made an intentional choice to consider others.** Daniel and I ended up at a restaurant with menus written in Serbian. Having too many dietary restrictions to risk playing point-and-pray roulette, we almost gave up. But then I pulled out my laptop, and—thanks to free wifi— we spent 20 minutes watching the wonders of Google Translate at work.

At one point, while Google was mid-translation, the phrase *angry peppers* appeared on the screen. Daniel and I looked at each other in bafflement. *Since when do peppers have emotions?* Then Google corrected itself: *cayenne pepper.* We snorted, then burst into much-needed laughter.

"You know," I said after we'd placed our orders, "this is what our English Language Learner students experience every single day, all year long. Sure, they have electronic translators. But they're slow, and often inaccurate. If today has been hard for us as adults, what must it be like for teenagers to spend a whole year where they're still learning the language?"

These five steps had immediate and long-term benefits. While in the airport, I was able to process an onslaught of powerful emotions in mature, healthy ways. And now, years later, I have great memories of the trip. I don't think of it as *that terrible time we got stranded in Serbia* but as *that rewarding week we spent in Serbia.*

But Sometimes We Really Are "Too Sensitive"

A Buzzfeed article titled "If You've Done 21/31 of These Things, You're Highly Sensitive" includes the following litmus test. It says you know you're an HSP if you have:

- cried at an ad
- cried at an ad that wasn't even particularly sad
- cried because someone complimented you
- cried because you were complimenting someone and became overwhelmed by how wonderful they are

- cried because someone asked you if you were crying
- went to the [bathroom] so you can have a nice cry in peace
- cried during an argument because it was stressful, then cried more out of frustration because someone told you to stop being so emotional

Clearly, this is tongue-in-cheek click-bait, not science. Sadly, articles like this reinforce negative stereotypes about HSPs. Crying doesn't make you a Highly Sensitive Person; crying is just one possible outcome of being overstimulated. We're not a bunch of crybabies. We don't fall to pieces at the first twinge of emotion. But sometimes we really *are* too sensitive. Hard as it may be to hear, this is a valid concern that we can't dismiss lightly. We can get so caught up in the intensity of our own "emotional vividness" that we can overwhelm the non-HSPs around us. Or, we can become so involved in experiencing others' emotions (which we'll discuss in chapter 16) that it can seem like we have lost touch with reality.

How can you tell when you are moving into "too sensitive" territory? Let's look at three common red flags.

1. Misinterpreting Motives

The first signal that you might be broaching "too sensitive" territory is that you misinterpret motives when you analyze someone's intentions based on what it would mean for you to do what they did (or say what they said) instead of checking directly with them to find out what they really meant.

Years ago, when I received an email from an acquaintance (we'll call her Carol) inviting me to attend a card-making class with her, I was elated. I'd secretly been wanting to become better friends with her, and here was the perfect opportunity! I showed up to class ten minutes early. As women asked if they could sit next to me, I proudly told them, "No, I'm saving this seat for a friend." Class started, no Carol. Fifteen minutes into class, I could feel women staring at the empty seat next to me. Finally, just as I'd given up, Carol rushed in, a full 30 minutes late. I smiled and pointed to the seat I'd defended for her, but she didn't notice; instead, she asked the instructor for a supply kit, waved at me, spun on a heel, and left.

I was stunned and stricken. For the rest of class, I struggled to contain my tears. When I got back in my car, they poured out the entire way home. How could she treat me like this? I'd been so excited by her invitation...then, it occurred to me: Maybe—just maybe—I'd misread her original message. Sure enough, when I pulled up her email, all it said was, "Cheri, I think you'd enjoy this class." I had supplied the additional subtext, partly because I wanted us to be friends, but mostly because if I had sent a message like that, I would have meant, "I'd really like to take this class with you."

Thank goodness I discovered my mistake quickly and didn't make it worse by either (a) spending my days moping about why Carol didn't value me the way I valued her or (b) melting down over how rude she'd been and how badly she'd disappointed me. That said, I must confess that I've had both responses—the "mope-about" and the "meltdown"—far too many times to count. They are both indications that I really am being too sensitive: over-focused on my own perspective and under-aware of the other person's point of view.

2. Getting Hung Up on How

For decades, my husband used to come into the kitchen and gripe, saying, "All I want is a clean knife, but noooo, they're all in the dishwasher! Why does everyone use so many knives? It's ridiculous. If you'd all just rinse it off after you use it..." For years, every time he complained about the knives, I felt personally attacked, as if he was criticizing how I fulfilled my role as kitchen coordinator. I'd bristle and defend myself by fault-finding in return.

A few years ago, as I was learning de-escalation techniques to help me metabolize my intense emotions in healthy ways, I wondered, "When he complains about the knives, I become so overwhelmed by his tone, I don't really hear his message. What is he actually trying to communicate?" That evening, the old scenario played out again in the kitchen. Lo and behold, I heard him actually saying, "I want a clean knife." I bought a new cutlery set, which doubled the number of knives in the kitchen, and he hasn't complained about knives since.

When we stew over someone's tone of voice more than we focus on their message, we're getting "hung up on how." The solution is two-fold. First, recognize that nobody can actually hear how their voice sounds to other people. Our superior temporal sulcus—the part of the brain that hears and interprets tone of voice—turns off when we speak, so when someone says, "What do you mean you don't like my tone?" they aren't necessarily being dismissive. There's a good chance they honestly have no idea what we're talking about.[4]

Second, focus on the "why" and the "what" before the "how." This can be challenging for HSPs, as we are so quick to pick up on tone, but it pays to investigate further before taking offense. When I asked myself, "Why does Daniel keep bringing up the knife issue?" I realized it was because he genuinely wanted to find a solution. While I didn't appreciate his *how*, his *why* and *what* were sound.

Why not tell people how their tone of voice is affecting you so they can change? You can certainly give it a try. Some people may be receptive. But the truth is, most people aren't nearly as tone sensitive as you are. If it's a deal-breaker,[5] set a firm boundary. If not, change what you can: your own approach.

3. Withdrawing Too Much

After spending the first 45 years of my life trying to convince other people I was just like everyone else, I gladly traded my faux "normal" badge in for an HSP banner. At first, every new act of self-advocacy felt like freedom. I was free to use unscented laundry detergent, free to cut the tags off my clothes, free to wear earplugs on the plane, free to leave a party early, free to ask the maitre d' to reseat us away from the entrance, and free to stay home and rest up.

But as the months turned into years, and without me realizing it was happening, some of that initial advocacy morphed into license. In the name of freedom, I gave myself permission to do whatever felt best in the moment. Sure, it seemed a bit odd when friends practically fell over themselves to tell me, "Cheri! It's so good to see you at church!"

but I didn't dwell on it. Not until I sat down with a calendar did I realize that "I'll just stay home today" had turned into "I'll just stay home this month" and was rapidly becoming "I'll just stay home this year."

Dr. Elaine Aron cautions HSPs not to over-avoid stimulation, because "the more we avoid stimulation, the more unpleasantly arousing the remaining stimulation becomes."[6] In my case, each time I opted to stay home for "self-care" instead of going out for a social gathering, I became more comfortable with an increasingly reclusive lifestyle.

When you notice yourself misinterpreting motives, getting hung up on the how, or withdrawing too much, create space, pause, and look up. In the midst of your too sensitive moments, receive God's comfort: his strength, in you.

14

The Exhaustion of High-Energy Events

Creating a Space for Rest and Renewal

Denise

I grew up in Northern California, and the men in my family were big-time fans of the San Francisco 49ers. At least once every fall, my dad would take us kids to a game. The three-hour drive from our small town to the big city was always a fun family adventure. I spent the entire trip in the back of our little red Datsun 210 station wagon. And when I say "the back," I mean the hatchback area. My brothers filled the backseats, so the hatchback was my designated area. Obviously, this was before seatbelt laws, but I had my own blanket and pillow and I loved having my own private space.

Given my shy tendencies as a kid, you would think a professional football game would overwhelm me. Few things are louder than 70,000 fans screaming after a touchdown, with all of them stomping and making your seat vibrate. An NFL game is nothing if not loud, colorful, and full of motion. And yet, I loved them.

Those football games are some of my fondest childhood memories. So why did an Easter dress cause me so much discomfort and a friend's slumber party wear me out, but a noisy, over-stimulating football game seem so fun?

One time my mom picked me up from my friend's birthday party and I wished the five-minute drive home from my friend's house could be as long as the drive home from San Francisco. I wanted a whole three hours in the back of our car—in my own quiet space, alone with my thoughts. That was the difference between two very outgoing and highly social experiences. The football game had a large built-in buffer of time both before and after the event. The party at a friend's house didn't.

I figured out early on that I love long drives, in part because they give me time to think about the event I just attended. By the time I'd arrive home, I was ready for the next thing. If I spent several hours at a friend's party or some other social event and I didn't have a long drive home, I knew I'd need to be alone in my bedroom for a while. I didn't know why this buffer of time was so helpful. I didn't even have the language yet to call it a "buffer of time" or a "time of transition," I simply knew I needed more time than my brothers or my friends before I could engage in the next activity. I needed time alone, in a quiet place, to process my recent experiences. I didn't know anything about Sensory Processing Sensitivity back then, but this space of time was a key way I learned to embrace what I considered "my inner weird."

The Benefits of Solitude

While I used to think my need for time alone was weird, I now think of it as essential. In today's hyper-connected world, it has become increasingly difficult to carve out time from our jam-packed schedules, and in those few intermittent moments when we're not busy, our phones continue beeping with messages and notifications.

> TIME TO THINK, PROCESS, AND UNWIND IS ESSENTIAL TO OUR PHYSICAL, EMOTIONAL, AND SPIRITUAL HEALTH.

True solitude has become something of a lost art. And yet, time to think, process, and unwind is essential to our physical, emotional, and spiritual health. This is true for HSPs and non-HSPs alike, but HSPs are prone to feeling additional strain in their lives when they neglect this important aspect of healthy living.

Times of solitude have become a rare commodity in our society and will not come to us automatically, but if we're to experience the fullness of all life has to offer, periods of solitude must be pursued with intention. Solitude is not antisocial or a mere preference for self-serving isolation; rather, time alone accomplishes several things:

1. Time alone enables us to process our experiences and achieve greater clarity about them.

2. Time alone allows our minds to consider potential solutions without external pressure.

3. Time alone increases our productivity by reducing distractions.

4. Time alone increases our creativity by giving our minds time to explore new ideas.

5. Time alone creates the space we need to consider and articulate our convictions.

6. Time alone gives us permission to downshift into a lower gear, which helps to restore us physically and mentally.

7. Time alone is one of the best ways to connect with God through Scripture and prayer.

8. Time alone allows us to return to our loved ones refreshed and able to love and serve them better.

For all the benefits solitude affords us, the purpose of seeking time alone is not for the sake of time alone itself. We seek a period of time away so we can return a healthier version of ourselves to serve those we love.

Setting Aside Time to Be Alone

Jesus is our primary example of the need to seek time away. During his earthly life, he continuously pursued time alone so he could pray, be refilled, and then return to the many people who sought him for healing and teaching. He often rose early in the morning to have this time alone (Mark 1:35), and he liked to finish a busy day by retreating in the evenings to a private place (Matthew 14:23). This was his pattern—to withdraw to someplace quiet—especially before and after he spent a day with a large crowd of people (Luke 5:16).

> JESUS IS OUR PRIMARY EXAMPLE OF THE
> NEED TO SEEK TIME AWAY.

Today, we can follow his example. When we know we're going to spend time around a lot of people in an overstimulating environment, we can pause and look up, and we can follow Christ's example to seek time alone either for prayer or for rest and renewal. HSPs are not fragile creatures who can't handle large crowds and high-octane events. We can attend concerts in stadiums and professional football games—and enjoy them!—when we understand and embrace the importance of giving ourselves some much-needed time to transition between activities.

Here are few ideas for being more intentional about creating times of solitude:

1. Begin with shorter, more manageable periods of time by setting aside 10-20 minutes a day when you can be alone. If that's too much, then start with five minutes a day.

2. Try getting up a few minutes earlier. Or, take a few minutes before bed to quiet your heart and mind with a few minutes alone.

3. Once a week (or more!) use your lunch break for some much-needed time alone.

4. Do not be surprised if time alone feels awkward at first. It takes time to strengthen our capacity to truly be alone with ourselves.

5. Silence your electronics to minimize distractions.

6. Schedule longer stretches of time alone on your calendar. Try a one-hour block and go from there.

7. Set aside a full day for time alone, whether for resting or goal-planning or both.

To enjoy those high-intensity events, HSPs need two things: 1) HSPs need to set aside time to rest and think, and 2) they need a quiet, calming space where they can do just that.

Creating a Space of Grace

As a kid I loved spending time in my bedroom. It was my private refuge where I could savor the uninterrupted quiet of my books and craft projects. Nowadays, I like to have a spare room where I can create my own little sanctuary, but whenever that's not possible, I have always designated a corner in my home that is my personal retreat. I call it my space of grace. It's where I go when I need a few moments—or more— to collect my thoughts and reorient my feelings.

I'm a big advocate for creating your own space of grace, and it doesn't have to cost a lot of money either. In fact, the essentials don't have to cost anything at all. Here are some tips for creating your own personal refuge on a budget.

Here is what you can do for free:

- Select a room or a corner of your home for your space of grace.
- Take a minimalist approach.
- Clear the space of any clutter.
- Keep all surfaces clean.
- Designate it a "kid-free" and "pet-free" zone.
- Eliminate any clashing colors.
- Hide electrical cords as much as possible, like the ones for lamps.

- Remove potential distractions like TVs, computers, and phones.
- Give every item a home of its own so you'll always know where everything goes.
- Allow natural sunlight to enter the room.
- Open a window for fresh air.
- Use a rain app for nature sounds.
- Create a playlist of your favorite instrumental music.
- Move your most comfortable chair and favorite piece of furniture into this space.
- Keep a space open on the floor for stretching.
- Keep your favorite personal items close by, like hand lotion or lip balm.
- Include your favorite family photos.
- Include your favorite books.
- Include a favorite journal and pen.
- Keep your Bible within reach.

Here is what you can do with minimal cost:

- Add a few soft blankets and pillows.
- Add a soft rug.
- Find a lamp with three-way lighting.
- Use warm-white bulbs with lower wattage.
- Hang a strand of white Christmas lights.
- Add a few candles, and consider using the battery-operated kind.
- Add a green plant in a favorite pot.
- Add fresh flowers in a mason jar.

- Create a warm, pleasing aroma by baking.
- Create a clean, fresh aroma by boiling water with a sliced lemon and a few cloves and cinnamon sticks.
- Add something quirky just for fun like a mug with a silly saying or a calendar with funny pictures.
- Use storage solutions that double as furniture, like a storage ottoman.
- Use plastic storage containers for under the bed or in the closet.

Here is what you can do with a little more investment:

- Paint the walls in soft white or light gray or perhaps a muted tone in a soothing color.
- Select wall art or photography that makes you smile.
- Use wooden crates or woven baskets for storage containers that are visible.
- Use a wireless speaker for your music.
- Add a small desktop fountain or aquarium.
- Use noise-canceling earphones.
- Find a really comfortable chair you'll enjoy spending time in.
- Add a minifridge or a coffee maker.
- Have a dimmer switch installed.

HSPs don't have to avoid those high-energy events. We simply need a place to retreat when it's all over, and our refuge doesn't need to cost a small fortune. The simpler, the better.

While HSPs are known to tire more easily from having so much to process, HSPs can still enjoy the same outings as their non-HSP friends, but it helps to prepare for these outings with some intentional time alone, either beforehand or afterward or both. And having your space of grace ready makes this not only possible, but also deeply satisfying.

15

The Weariness of Worship
Enjoying Both Community and Solitude in Liturgy
Denise

M y earliest memories are of me sitting on the front pew at church, watching my mom lead the congregation in worship. She held a microphone in one hand and a tambourine in the other. The way she could sing and shake that thing in rhythmic timing fascinated me, but I never liked the shrill sound of its jingles. I was always glad when the fast songs ended and the slow songs began. Slow songs meant no more tambourine.

Our brand of Sunday morning worship took Psalm 98:4 seriously, which says, "Make a joyful noise unto the LORD, all the earth: make a loud noise, and rejoice, and sing praise" (KJV). I knew all about the loud noise of worship. It included lots of clapping while shouting, "Amen!" As a child, this was all I knew, so I assumed this was simply "how worship was done." Then, as a young adult, I began visiting different churches with friends.

The first time I attended a Catholic Mass, the formality of the service struck me as both austere and beautiful in a serious and reverent sort of way. I liked it the way a person likes to visit someplace new, but it didn't quite feel like home. Then I visited a Baptist church. This worship service felt similar to what I was used to, but calmer and without the shouting.

Truth be told, I felt a little like Goldilocks visiting the home of the three bears. One church was too loud. Another was too serious. But eventually I found one that was just right. I know this makes me sound like a consumer shopping for a church, but I was young, exploring my faith, and trying to figure out what I believed on my own, and part of that process was visiting different churches.

When I moved to Southern California in my early twenties, I attended Lake Avenue Congregational Church in Pasadena and discovered yet another style of worship. The sanctuary seats 3,000 people, which is almost as many people as the population of the entire town I was raised in, but more than the size of the church, the worship service moved me. Sometimes we sang hymns, but other times a full orchestra played pieces by Bach or Beethoven. These moments of instrumental music allowed for a time of reflection and prayer. Until then, I had no idea some churches played music like that! Oh, how I loved it. My soul responded in worship with a kind of deep gratitude that could not be expressed with shouts of hallelujah.

Being an HSP in a Non-HSP Church World

A comprehensive analysis of various worship styles throughout church history is worthy of its own book-length treatment. In all likelihood, you and I have had different experiences when it comes to church life in general and worship services in particular. Maybe for you attending a weekend worship service is a sweet respite from a harried week of constant noise and endless demands. Or maybe a Sunday morning church service is just one more thing you feel you must do, but it leaves you feeling drained.

One thing I have noticed about HSPs after they've discovered they're HSPs is an intentional avoidance of environments that are overstimulating, and sometimes this includes church. If the weekend worship service they attend is too loud or too demonstrative or too whatever, they opt out, preferring to stay home and watch the sermon online. I know because I've done this myself.

In recent years, my husband and I chose to attend a large church in our neighborhood, where our kids could see the same friends at school they see at church. We appreciated the teaching, but the music wasn't my cup of tea. After a while, I started to show up for church late—on purpose—to avoid the rock concert with the smoke machines and laser lights. It wasn't just the style of music either. It was everything from the mandatory handshakes with the over-eager greeters at the door to the obligatory meet-and-greet in the middle of the service where you're expected to engage in small talk with those around you.

The "worship" there wore me out. I knew I could prepare for a highly stimulating event by resting before and after the service, but that seemed to defeat the purpose of going to church in the first place. Soon, it became easier to stay home and tune in online. For the first time in my life, I was "skipping Sunday" to savor a quiet morning with my Bible and my favorite cup of tea. But this was in direct conflict with what I believe, not because there's anything wrong with reading the Bible and drinking tea, but because we as believers are called to be a part of a larger body—the body of Christ—and we can't do that very well when we're home alone in our own private sanctuary.

If something about church, and about me as an HSP, makes me want to skip church entirely, then that's a pretty good indicator I'm not connected to the body of Christ the way I need to be, and I need to do something different. For me, that meant finding a neighborhood church where I could be a full participant—without getting a headache.

Enjoying Both Community and Solitude in Liturgy

I cherish times of solitude. I look forward to those moments each day when I can curl up in my favorite chair with the Good Book, and I enjoy writing out my prayers in a journal. These times of quiet nourish my soul the way cool water quenches a deep thirst. At the same time, I also recognize that while prayer and Bible study are core spiritual disciplines, there is more to the Christian life than being home alone with my Bible and pen. We fill up so we can pour out.

In her book *Quiet*, Susan Cain shares a candid conversation with Adam McHugh who wrote *Introverts in the Church*. McHugh says that when he became active in evangelicalism, "he began to feel guilty about all that solitude. He even believed that God disapproved of his choices, and by extension, of him."[1] To put it another way, when the church culture emphasizes community and the need for everyone to be involved in community groups, this may feel at odds with someone who genuinely enjoys significant stretches of solitude. For McHugh, this tension led to a "sense of spiritual failure."[2]

> WE FILL UP SO WE CAN POUR OUT.

I have great empathy for anyone who struggles with the tension between desiring time alone and time with others. For many HSPs, this is a regular, if not daily, occurrence. The church's emphasis on community, however, dates back to the earliest days of Christendom. Acts 2:46 says, "Every day they continued to meet together in the temple courts. They broke bread in their homes and ate together with glad and sincere hearts." The early church did life together as a natural part of their weekly—even daily—rhythms, so it's understandable that churches today want to maintain this sense of community.

From the beginning, community has been God's idea. When God made man, he famously said, "It is not good for the man to be alone" (Genesis 2:18). Even before that, God existed for eternity past in perfect community within the Trinity of Father, Son, and Spirit. To be in community is biblical. In fact, God goes even further and calls this community his family! The whole premise of the Bible is that God gave his Son to die on the cross so that we could be called his sons and daughters (2 Corinthians 6:18). We are more than a community; we are a family. And healthy families require time spent together.

So how do those of us who feel a strong pull toward times of solitude reconcile this with the biblically based importance of church community?

Community and solitude do not have to be pitted against one another as an either/or choice. We can embrace both as part of the natural ebb and flow of a healthy Christian life. As mentioned in chapter 14, a time of solitude is great preparation for rejoining a larger group of people. We can serve others better when we have first spent time alone with God. Moreover, a weekend worship service is a chance once every seven days to pause and look up, to focus our eyes on Christ. Attending church and embracing the fellowship of other believers is part of the weekly rhythm that reminds us why we're here—to love God and love others. As HSPs, we can see our need for periodic solitude as a healthy complement to the church's rightful emphasis on community.

> HSPs NEED BOTH COMMUNITY AND
> PERIODIC TIMES OF SOLITUDE.

Where McHugh felt a sense of spiritual failure for desiring so much solitude, I have felt the opposite. Rather than feeling like a spiritual failure, I have felt the need to guard against becoming spiritually prideful for enjoying so much quiet time alone with God. This is where I feel closest to God, when I'm alone with him in his Word. My desire for solitude comes easier for me than other things, like the dreaded meet-and-greet on Sunday mornings. And yet, I recognize the beauty of gathering with God's people, as I'm sure McHugh does, too.

Both extremes should be avoided: thinking God is displeased with us because of our desire for solitude or thinking we are somehow spiritually superior because of it. We need both community and periodic times of solitude.

Where I'll Be on Sunday

For a long time I was taught that "bigger is better" when it comes to worship. By "bigger," I mean more visibly demonstrative. Clapping hard. Raising hands. Shouting "hallelujah!" Today, I freely admit I prefer quieter forms of worship. I enjoy times of silence when I can focus my thoughts on God's Word and his attributes. I also savor those moments when I can lift my voice in unison with those around me and sing of his faithfulness. A person's preference in worship style will, of course, depend on several factors beyond just being an HSP, not the least of which is his or her doctrinal beliefs.

Since HSPs are less apt to enjoy anything loud, much less loud worship, you and I might find ourselves drawn to worship styles that are somewhat softer in expression. In this case, a liturgical or traditional service might be a good fit. At the same time, it's important that we leave room for the fact that individual churches express their worship in different ways. The variety of churches and worship styles in North America is seemingly limitless, and when you think about Christians around the world who are persecuted for their faith, it's almost embarrassing to have so many choices available to us.

This coming Sunday I'll attend a worship service with my family like we do every week. We now attend a church that holds three services; two of them are considered contemporary and one of them is more traditional. I am incredibly thankful I live in a country where there are so many churches with differing worship styles available. Not every Christian around the world can say the same thing.

For some believers, they gather and worship knowing that at any moment they could be arrested—even executed—for their faith. The volume of the speaker system is the least of their concerns, so if my own Sunday morning service is a little too loud for my taste, or the meet-and-greet a little too long, I accept these realities as the blessings they are, for they mean I live in a country that allows me to worship God without fear. And that's reason enough to shout a hearty, "Hallelujah!"

16

The Complexity of Caring

Embracing Empathy Without Buckling Under the Sorrow

Cheri

No pennies! No pennies!"

Annemarie, age three, has been playing quietly on the family room floor for an hour. Without warning, she throws her toys, grabs her blankie, and begins to wail.

"No pennies! I have no pennies!"

I rush to sit beside her on the floor, scoop her into my lap, and begin to croon. "It's okay, Chickie. It's okay." Experience has taught me that her sobs will crescendo before subsiding, so I hunker down so we can weather the storm together.

"No pennies!" Annemarie declares again between jagged breaths.

What is she talking about? I wonder. *Why is money suddenly...*I stop rocking and stare at her in disbelief. Did she overhear my phone call? An hour earlier, I'd been talking with a bank customer service representative, trying to figure out why our checking account is—once again—overdrawn. I had done the math so carefully this time. I knew we would be close to zero, but I was certain we would not be in the red.

As the detached voice at the other end of the line advised me to simply visit any local branch to make a deposit before the close of business in order to avoid incurring further NSF (Non-Sufficient Funds) charges, I had burst into tears and blurted, "I have no money!"

Glancing into the next room where Annemarie played unperturbed, I had lowered my voice to a hoarse croak. "I have no money!" I thought I had shielded her, but clearly, she'd heard me after all. She's far too young, of course, to comprehend exactly what it meant, but she understands I'm upset. As I rock and whisper, "It's okay, Chickie. It's okay," into my little girl's unruly curls, I realize: She absorbed my emotions—with astonishing accuracy.

A Day in the Life of an HSP

I am guessing you could tell similar stories of your own about times when you've unintentionally picked up someone else's emotions. This tendency to automatically empathize with others is one of the key pieces of the HSP puzzle.[1] When you empathize with someone, you don't merely imagine how you might feel if you were in their shoes. That's sympathy. Empathy goes deeper. Empathy's prefix *em–* means "in," and its root word *pathos* means "feeling." When HSPs empathize, our own emotions begin to mirror the emotions of the other person—even if they haven't said a word.

> WHEN HSPs EMPATHIZE, OUR OWN EMOTIONS BEGIN TO MIRROR THE EMOTIONS OF THE OTHER PERSON.

As an HSP you're an expert at "reading the room" in a social setting, too. You know that the couple three tables away is fighting, even though they're still smiling. You heave a sigh of sadness and feel a wave of loneliness as you look away from them. You can tell your waitress has been crying and is trying valiantly not to tear up while she takes your order. Not wanting to burst her dam by asking, "Are you okay?" you add extra warmth to your voice and leave a generous tip. You sense the new acquaintance seated next to you has received good news that she'd love to share with someone, so you ask, "What's the best thing that's happened to you this week?" and spend the next 20 minutes nodding and smiling. And all of that in one short hour at IHOP!

These occurrences are a normal part of an HSP's everyday reality.

While some non-HSPs must consciously work at *perspective-taking*—recognizing points of view other than their own—this comes naturally to a Highly Sensitive Person. Being emotionally perceptive and receptive is in our DNA.

The Science of Empathy and Mirror Neurons

The HSP brain is hardwired to notice people and enter into their emotions. In brain imaging studies, numerous areas of the brain associated with real time awareness light up when Highly Sensitive Persons view pictures of people, and the response is even stronger if the people depicted are in a social situation or exhibiting a strong emotion.[2] While many non-HSPs are able to ignore people around them, tuning people out is not an easy option for HSPs. Quite the opposite. We're more likely to stay on "high alert" the entire time we're at a social gathering, constantly scanning, reading, and responding to everyone in the room.[3]

Imagine these people-perceiving parts of your HSP brain as sportscasters. When you're out and about, they're busy announcing the players, filling in their backstories, analyzing key moves and microexpressions, zooming in close then panning back out, hitting instant replay, making predictions, and reacting in amazement. All this automatic activity happens nonstop the entire time you're in a social setting. As one writer aptly puts it, "If you're an HSP, other people are the brightest thing on your radar."[4]

As an HSP, you're not just noticing people; your brain is constantly analyzing their behavior so you can understand who they are and why they do what they do. This keeps your mirror neurons far busier than those of non-HSPs. Mirror neurons play a vital role in compassion and empathy. When you notice someone doing (or feeling) something in the here and now, your mirror neurons compare and connect it to your memories of similar actions (or emotions) in your own past.[5]

Think of your mirror neurons as actors and set designers in a complex simulation game. They work together to create a vicarious experience that's very realistic. If you cry at social media videos of soldiers returning home from duty, it's because your mirror neurons are hard at work, helping you not only to imagine what the overjoyed spouses, children, and dogs might be feeling but to experience their surprise, amazement, relief, gratitude, and joy yourself.

Empathy can also be unexpectedly isolating. The way you read people enables you to connect with them quickly, and some folks may bond to you as their new best friend during the first five minutes of conversation. But you can tell that the empathy isn't mutual in most of your relationships. You are quick to understand others, but few people really resonate with you. Most of your relationships may feel one-sided, lacking reciprocity. You often feel lonely because you're not experiencing empathetic attunement.

As you might expect, empathy can also be overwhelming. While most people's mirror neurons work the equivalent of 9-5 jobs, yours never really clock out. Constant empathy means you're like a super-absorbent emotional sponge, so to keep from becoming saturated with emotions that are not yours to carry, you need to be wrung out regularly.

When your empathy starts to feel isolating or overwhelming, you need to create space to pause and look up. Hand others' emotions over to God in empathetic surrender and receive your Father's reassurance: *I'm here. You're not alone. We're in this together.*

Remove or Reduce

As HSPs we pick up other people's emotions from our surroundings the same way our boots pick up mud when we walk through a field after a storm. You wouldn't think of wearing your muddy boots into the house, or propping them up on the coffee table, or leaving them on when you climb into bed. No way! You would remove your boots outside, hose them down, and leave them outside to dry. And yet, HSPs are oftentimes oblivious to the way our emotion-encrusted hearts leave muddy prints and dirt trails all over our homes and relationships.

As HSPs, we can and must learn healthy ways of dealing with the many feelings we pick up. What we do naturally, however, is hold onto and ruminate over the emotions that cling to us, which quickly becomes a burden for us and a barrier to others. So, we must be intentional about regularly taking off our emotionally muddy boots, hosing them down, and leaving them outside your heart to dry. Sometimes, this means removing yourself—along with all your over-active mirror neurons—from the situation entirely. This might look like:

- walking out of the movie that's giving you a sick feeling in the pit of your stomach, and a glance at your watch tells you there's still half an hour to go

- exiting the friendly discussion that's morphing into a terse debate

- getting off the phone as soon as you recognize that someone's "venting" is not helping them and only hurting you

"Oh, I can't do that!" you say. "What if they...?" Let me interrupt right there. I cannot tell you exactly what to do in every situation, but I can tell you that if your gut reaction to taking care of your empathetic HSP heart is, "What if they...?" then you're asking the wrong question.

The right question is, "When will I...?" As in, "At what point will I choose to remove myself from a situation that's causing empathy overload?" Another good question is, "How will I...?" As in, "How will I remove myself in a way that respects everyone involved?" And also, "Who pays the highest price when I stay?"

You already know, of course, the answer to the last question. Who pays the highest price when I stay? First you, and then everyone you come into contact with. When you overstay, your empathy corrodes into resentment. According to research by Dr. Brené Brown, "The most compassionate people...have the most well-defined and well-respected boundaries."[6] Sometimes, the best way to use your God-given empathy is to leave.

If it is not possible or practical to remove yourself from a situation that is causing empathy overload, try reducing your exposure. Set a time limit with a cell phone app or an old-fashioned kitchen timer. When the alarm goes off, be done—at least for now.

Your friends can finish the movie; you'll be waiting for them in the café. The debate can continue another day, another time. You are done for today. The chaos-creators in your life do not *need* to keep spewing negativity in your presence in order to move on. The venting myth ("I have to let off steam or else I'll blow") was debunked years ago;[7] although co-ruminating (talking excessively about problems with others) can make you feel more connected to others, it raises your stress levels[8] and traps you in Unhealthy HSP Mode. If all else fails, find a pair of earplugs or noise-canceling headphones. Keep them nearby to aid you in lessening the impact when you aren't able to leave.

Removing yourself and reducing your exposure will not earn you popularity points in the short run, but that's okay. The truth, as Dr. Brené Brown reports from her research, is that "compassionate people ask for what they need. They say no when they need to, and when they say yes, they mean it. They are compassionate because their boundaries keep them out of resentment."[9]

> THE SAME BOUNDARIES THAT KEEP YOU FROM BEING OVERWHELMED ALSO KEEP YOUR EMPATHY STRONG IN HEALTHY WAYS.

Let that last sentence really sink in: "They are compassionate because their boundaries keep them out of resentment." This is especially true for you as an HSP. The same boundaries that keep you from being overwhelmed by other people's emotions also keep your empathy strong in healthy ways.

Moving from Feelings to Action

The fact that HSPs are hardwired for empathy is a double-edged sword. On the one hand, our tender hearts can become isolated and overwhelmed by our own empathetic zeal. On the other hand, our deep compassion motivates us to reach out to people, to which we will devote all of Part Three.

Through it all, remember: You are not alone. Take heart knowing that your empathetic Savior understands: "For we do not have a high priest who is unable to empathize with our weaknesses, but we have one who has been tempted in every way, just as we are—yet he did not sin" (Hebrews 4:15). As you learn healthy ways to handle your empathy, this God-given gift will become a powerful tool for serving others and sharing Christ's love.

Part Three

Looking Out

In humility value others above yourselves,
not looking to your own interests
but each of you to the interests of others.

PHILIPPIANS 2:3-4

The Gift of Self-Forgetfulness
Breaking Free from Hyper Self-Awareness
Denise

Hold on, I need to check something," I tell my husband before step-ping into the car. Something has been irritating my back all morn-ing, and despite earlier attempts to find the source of my discomfort, I try again. I reach around my back and from inside my shirt, I pull out a single strand of hair. "There! See?" I hold up the fine filament of hair for my husband to see. "I knew something was bugging me."

"Why am I not surprised you could feel that?" my husband asks dryly.

By now he's used to my idiosyncrasies. When we're getting ready to leave the house, he knows I can't go anywhere without my sunglasses. Direct sunlight is too blinding. When we're in a theater, he knows I can't focus on the movie when the person behind us keeps reaching inside a crinkly bag of chips. The noise is so distracting. And when I bring a new package of socks home from the store, he knows I want to wash them before I wear them because I don't like the store's smell on my new socks. I know, I'm weird. Peculiar. Or maybe just plain picky.

I don't like these things about myself. I wish my eyes weren't so sen-sitive to light. I wish I could tune out distracting noises. And I wish I could wear something as simple as new socks straight from the store without washing them in my own detergent first. But certain sights, sounds, and smells get to me. It's like I'm on high alert all the time, noticing things I wish I could ignore more easily.

I cannot count how many times I've said to my husband, "I'm sorry I'm so high maintenance. I don't want to be high maintenance."

He always comes back with, "Nah, you're just medium maintenance. Besides, I like that my princess can always find the pea."

We both laugh. Because that's what he calls me.

The Princess and the Pea

If you're not familiar with the fairy tale by Hans Christian Andersen, the plot follows a prince who can't find a princess because none of the possible women he has met possess the delicate manners suited for a princess. Then a young woman seeks shelter in the castle from a rainstorm. When she claims to be a princess, the prince's mother creates a test for the young woman and places a single pea beneath a pile of twenty feather mattresses. The next morning, the young woman mentions the terrible night's sleep she had (presumably because she could feel the "lump" in her bed), and the prince realizes she is a real princess.

Like the princess in the fairy tale, HSPs can almost always find the "pea," and at times this heightened sense of awareness can be helpful. If someone accidentally bumps the burner switch on the stove, I usually smell the gas before anyone else. If the car is making a barely audible rhythmic sound, I know to pull over and check the tires. One of them is probably low on air.

Such awareness, however, has its downside, too. When you are constantly aware of all the sights, sounds, and smells around you, then you are also aware of how those sights, sounds, and smells are affecting you. As you naturally process the various surrounding stimuli and consider its impact on you, your attention is drawn inward.

What begins as heightened awareness quickly leads to hyper self-awareness, which can settle into an ongoing feeling of self-consciousness. Pretty soon, an HSP's thoughts can become consumed with how everything in the environment is affecting them, either positively or negatively. HSPs can become disproportionately focused on themselves, and with an added measure of irony, HSPs may not even realize how extremely self-aware they've become. It's just their normal.

While some self-awareness can be good, especially in social settings where a certain etiquette is required, too much self-awareness is never a good thing. No one enjoys being around a person who is self-absorbed. So, if Sensory Processing Sensitivity leaves HSPs with a predisposition to heightened self-awareness, how can an HSP prevent that proclivity from becoming all-consuming? How can we be HSPs who seek to love and serve others and not be obsessed with how everything is affecting us?

The Gift of Self-Forgetfulness

One of the greatest gifts we can give to others is our presence—not only our physical presence, but our presence of mind and heart as well. And to be fully present with another person means we cannot be preoccupied with self.

> ONE OF THE GREATEST GIFTS WE CAN
> GIVE TO OTHERS IS OUR PRESENCE.

In all likelihood, we have all experienced what it is like to be with someone who is not fully present. After church one Sunday, I was having a conversation with a woman in leadership. I had been hoping to get to know her better, and we happened to cross paths in the courtyard. We stopped and chatted a while, and in an effort to connect with her, I tried to be more transparent and vulnerable, so I shared with her a struggle I'd been having. While I talked, I noticed her peering into my sunglasses as she adjusted her bangs. She wasn't listening to what I was saying; she was preening her hair with her reflection in my sunglasses.

While I would like to think I have never done that myself, I have to admit that sometimes I am in conversation with a person and deep down I am really thinking about the milk and bread I need to pick up from the store. We have all been there. We know what it is like to be physically present while mentally preoccupied with something else. This is why the gift of self-forgetfulness is so important.

In his book *The Freedom of Self-Forgetfulness*, Timothy Keller says the marks of a heart that has been radically transformed by God's grace are gospel-humility and self-forgetfulness.[1] He explains that "Gospel-humility is not needing to think about myself. Not needing to connect things with myself. It is an end to such thoughts as, 'I'm in this room with these people, does that make me look good? Do I want to be here?'"[2] Keller confronts a core issue all humans face. None of us enjoy talking with someone who is constantly looking over our shoulders to see who else they'd rather be talking to in the room. That kind of person is self-absorbed; he's only interested in using other people to make himself look good. He is entirely self-focused, the opposite of self-forgetful.

A self-forgetful person, however, is not concerned with how she looks or whom she's with or what others might be thinking about her. She isn't thinking about herself at all; she is sincerely focused on you and what you are saying. Whenever we walk away from talking to that kind of person, we know it inside. We can feel the difference. She has given us a gift—the gift of her full attention, telling us without so many words that we matter.

As HSPs we want to be that kind of friend, that kind of coworker, that kind of spouse, and that kind of parent. We want to break free from the hyper self-awareness that so easily becomes normative for us, and we want to embrace the beautiful gift of self-forgetfulness, so we can be fully present to others. Keller describes it like this:

> Friends, wouldn't you want to be a person who does not need honour—nor is afraid of it? Someone who does not lust for recognition—nor, on the other hand, is frightened to death of it? Don't you want to be the kind of person who, when they see themselves in a mirror or reflected in a shop window, does not admire what they see but does not cringe either?...Or perhaps you tend to beat yourself up and to be tormented by regrets. Wouldn't you like to be free of them?[3]

To be self-forgetful is to be unencumbered with thoughts of self, either good or bad. This kind of person is free from both self-aggrandizing thoughts and self-destructive thoughts. This kind of person is free to be fully present with others, fully engaged in what the other person is saying. Because this kind of person is not thinking about herself, she is a gift to everyone around her.

> TO BE SELF-FORGETFUL IS TO BE UNENCUMBERED
> WITH THOUGHTS OF SELF, EITHER GOOD OR BAD.

This is the gift of self-forgetfulness. This can be an HSP's reality, too. Our genetic disposition toward self-awareness does not mean we are doomed to a life of self-absorption. By God's grace, we can invite the Holy Spirit to empower us, not to think less of ourselves, but to think of ourselves less.[4]

We can be like John the Baptist. When more and more followers left him to follow Jesus, John's disciples were concerned with their decreasing popularity, but John was not focused on himself or his popularity. He considered it his greatest joy to step aside and let all the glory go to Jesus. That's when John the Baptist uttered these famous words, "He must become greater; I must become less" (John 3:30). John understood the gift of self-forgetfulness, and in a genuine act of selflessness, he pointed his own followers toward another.

We can make John the Baptist's words our own prayer. We can pray that Jesus will increase, and we will decrease. We can pray that our focus will be fixed on Christ, and not ourselves. We can pray that God will enable us to look not only to our own interests, but also to the interests of others (Philippians 2:4).

We do not have to be preoccupied with the ticking clock in the corner or the humming refrigerator in the background. We do not have to be so intently focused on how our world is affecting us. We can listen to the Holy Spirit to help us see the needs around us and consider the ways we might serve others. This is our aim for the remainder of Part Three:

- In chapter 18, we'll examine how we utilize our time and how we can be intentional to set aside time, so we are free to serve others.

- In chapter 19, we'll explore those places where we are uniquely equipped to help those who are experiencing similar hurts to our own, so we can speak life and hope to the new story Jesus can write.

- In chapter 20, we'll turn our attention to the sweetest gift any friend can give—being a good listener.

- In chapter 21, we'll focus on a different way to look at hospitality and the simple ways we can serve others.

- In chapter 22, we'll consider the various contexts for creativity and how we can be a blessing to others through the talents God has given us.

- In chapter 23, we'll look at the ways HSPs are poised to serve as leaders and use their influence in ways that are beneficial for everyone.

When we get outside of ourselves and look for ways we can serve, that is when we discover the greatest joy.

18

The Gift of Time
Saying Yes to Less So You Can Give More
Cheri

*H*ow does she do it all?
    Why can't I keep up with her?
What's wrong with me?

I'd been asking myself these questions for decades, comparing myself unfavorably to other women. But when my friend Kathi Lipp came up with a brilliant analogy that answered my questions, I didn't like the answer. Not one little bit.

You've probably heard the expression "I've got too much on my plate." Well, Kathi compares each woman's productivity capacity to a different plate size. Most women have an average-size dinner plate. Some have a big turkey platter. And then, there are those of us who have little demitasse saucers. It's taken me years to admit that no matter how hard I try to prove otherwise, I'm not a platter or even a plate kinda' gal. As an HSP, I'm a tiny saucer girl.

Oh, how I used to question God for giving me an itty-bitty saucer along with turkey platter-sized desires. *Why would you do this to me? If you had to give me such a teensy-weensy capacity, why couldn't you at least reduce my longings to match? Is this some kind of cruel joke?* I felt like the widow at Zarephath (1 Kings 17:12), looking in despair at her final handful of flour and tiny bit of remaining oil; with such meager capacity, surely my dreams were doomed to die.

A few years ago, I was whining to Kathi (once again) about how unfair it was for God to give me a saucer-sized capacity with platter-sized dreams. Kathi responded, "But I feel like you do have a platter. Truly. I know you don't, but it sure seems like it to the rest of us."

Our friend Angela added, "Cheri, you must have the largest saucer ever or maybe you have the cup and the saucer capacity put together."

Without thinking, I said, "Then God has got to be multiplying things somewhere along the way." I paused, as a new thought came to me: *Maybe this is when he can miraculously transform our little into much—when we accept what we have and quit trying to beg, borrow, and steal plates that aren't ours.*

The more I reflected on our conversation, the more I realized Kathi and Angela were right. As a Highly Sensitive Person, I do have a smaller-than-average capacity. But in spite of this, the past few years have been enormously productive for me, both in terms of service and satisfaction. I'm getting better at saying "no" to most things, and only saying "yes" when I am clear the Holy Spirit is leading me to.

HSPs and Time Management Needs

One of the top needs I hear from the HSPs I coach is help with time management. How many of these concerns sound familiar?

- I need more time to sleep and eat and rest than other people who have more stamina.

- I have never-ending to-do lists.

- I feel ridiculous because many people do so much more than I do and aren't that stressed about it.

- I always feel so far behind.

- I don't know where to start, so I spin in circles, getting nowhere but dizzy.

- I move slower than most people because I tend to be very thorough, I like having closure, and I am not good at multitasking.

- I give away too much of myself.

- I want to quit everything and hide.

- I give and give until I hit a wall.

- I have a hard time keeping up with what everyone wants me to do/be. I work myself into the ground to get things done. If you have a project, I'm your girl.

- I wear myself out and make myself and everyone else miserable because of trying so hard to please so many people. Then I crash and crash hard. And then I feel guilty for letting everyone down.

And how many of these oh-so-important questions sound familiar?

- *How do I help others without getting pressured into doing a lot of things I don't want to do?*

- *Is living like Jesus something I'll ever learn?*

- *What does "laying down self" really look like?*

- *How does it work when I do things for others but all the time I'm resenting it?*

I can't give you one-size-fits-all answers to these vital questions. What I can offer are six simple questions that help me listen for the Holy Spirit's guidance as I'm considering a new commitment.

The Six-Word, Six-Question Precommitment Prayer

Why Am I Doing This Now?
Why **Am** I Doing This Now?
Why Am **I** Doing This Now?
Why Am I **Doing** This Now?
Why Am I Doing **This** Now?
Why Am I Doing This **Now**?

The basic question is just six words long: *Why am I doing this now?* It can be prayed six different ways, each time with a different emphasis.

1. *Why* am I doing this now?

This is a simple *motivation* question. Often, the answer is quite surface. Let's say a friend invites me to meet her for lunch, and my knee-jerk reaction is to say, "Yes!" When praying, "*Why* am I doing this now?" it's easy for me to supply the answer rather than listening for the Holy Spirit: *It sounds like fun!* Simple question, simple answer, right? Not so fast: A simple answer often acts as a cover for the true answer.

2. Why *am* I doing this now?

This is a much deeper *purpose* question. Typically, the answer takes some digging. Sure, lunch with a friend sounds like fun. But when I enter into conversational prayer, asking "Why *am* I doing this now?" I might get the truthful response, "Because you're feeling overextended, and you're looking for an escape." With this kind of clarity, I need to find a healthier way to take a break, and schedule time with my friend later, when I can show up to serve her, not use her as an escape.

Or the Holy Spirit might remind me that I often say a knee-jerk "yes" because saying "no" to a possible commitment feels like I'm saying "no" to my connection with the person asking. In such a scenario, I need to remember that regardless of whether I say "yes" or "no" to a commitment, I can always say "yes" to connection.

> REGARDLESS OF WHETHER I SAY "YES" OR "NO"
> TO A COMMITMENT, I CAN ALWAYS SAY "YES"
> TO CONNECTION.

3. Why am *I* doing this now?

This is an *identity* question with two follow-up questions:

- Is this something *only* I can do?
- Or am *I* doing it because I'm lured by the idol of *productivity*, the idol of *being needed*, the idol of *human approval*, or the idol of *false peace*?

This question came in handy when I needed PowerPoint slides to publicize a local poetry contest to my students. I was about to spend an hour creating them, but when I prayed, "Why am *I* doing this?" the immediate answer was "Because you're a control freak" (the Holy Spirit tends to be rather blunt with me!).

I then asked, "Is this something *only* I can do?" to which the answer was clearly "no." I knew plenty of people who were perfectly capable of creating PowerPoint slides, most of them far better than I could. As I considered my options, the Holy Spirit brought to mind my student worker. *Oh, yeah! She won first prize in the last year's competition. She's the perfect person for the task!* Not only did she do a great job, but she was thrilled to be asked.

If you, too, happen to be a recovering control freak, generous delegation is a true act of service. Prayerfully consider who you can invite to contribute their gifts instead of insisting on doing everything yourself.

4. Why am I *doing* this now?

This is a *process* question. When I pray, "Why am I *doing* this now?" I'm asking the Holy Spirit whether *doing* is the right step for this project right now. Or, perhaps I should be researching, reflecting, resting, seeking counsel, asking for help, waiting, or backing away instead.

The Holy Spirit convicted me of my obsession with *doing, doing, doing* a few years ago as I read a blog post by Seth Godin.[1] Alluding to a scene from *The Hobbit* in which Bilbo Baggins says, "I feel thin...sort of stretched...like butter scraped over too much bread," Godin asked, "What happens if instead of always seeking more butter, we find the discipline to cover less bread?" That was painful enough to read, but then he twisted the knife. "Spreading our butter too thin is a form of hiding. It helps us be busy but makes it unlikely we will make an impact." When *doing* is my response to the Holy Spirit's leading, then it's the healthy choice. But *only* then. Otherwise, all my *doing, doing, doing* just makes me busy...and ineffective.

5. Why am I doing *this* now?

This is a *priority* question. Of all the things I could be doing, is *this* the best use of my time and energy? I have so many interests, and I love starting new things. So "whatever thy hand findeth to do" is a dangerous concept, because my hands findeth so many things to do!

Recently, Daniel and I agreed to spend the evening hours hanging out together. Then I started catching up on Facebook and laughing at all the funny photos my friends posted. I kept 5-more-minuting my husband until the Holy Spirit reminded me to pray, "Why am I doing *this* now?" Which gave me a much-needed wake-up call. I had a ready opportunity to serve my husband with my time and attention, yet I was frittering away my time on Facebook. Time to reprioritize, pronto!

6. Why am I doing this *now*?

This is a *timing* question. When I pray, "Why am I doing this *now?*" I'm seeking a green light to move forward, a yellow light to slow down, or a red light to hit the brakes. Several years ago, I started the new year by excitedly diving into writing a book proposal. I was overwhelmed with urgency because a window of opportunity had finally opened: An agent I wanted to impress was suddenly accepting new queries. But several hours in, I paused to prayerfully ask, "Why am I doing this *now?* I have grading to do, retreat talks to revise, a house to clean, and...and...!"

Immediately, I knew that I needed to hit the "Save" button and put the book proposal on my calendar six months down the road. It was a *this* the Holy Spirit was leading me to do, just not *now*. Prayerfully asking, "Why am I doing this *now?*" helped me realize that I already had enough on my plate. I had preexisting commitments to people the Holy Spirit had previously called me to serve, and I needed to fulfill those commitments before starting new ones.

Why am I doing this now?	motivation
Why **am** I doing this now?	purpose
Why am **I** doing this now?	identity
Why am I **doing** this now?	process
Why am I doing **this** now?	priority
Why am I doing this **now**?	timing

Living like Jesus, laying down self, and serving others with joy all result from following the Holy Spirit's leading. When considering a new commitment, pray the six simple questions within the six-word prayer, then listen for the Holy Spirit's guidance.

The Gift of a Tiny Saucer

When I speak about plate sizes during a women's retreat, I invite three volunteers to come up front and hold an actual dinner plate, turkey platter, and demitasse saucer for the entire audience to see. After explaining plate size as a metaphor for personal capacity, I ask, "Which plate size is the best?" Without fail, the room erupts in shouts of, "The turkey platter!" It's a trick question, of course. The best plate size is the one God gave you.

Each time I pray the six-word prayer, I am surrendering my capacity back to God, trusting Him to do with it what He will. After so many years of trying to prove God wrong by pretending to have a turkey platter, I feel like I'm finally getting out of his way so he can work. And I now realize that God's promise to the widow at Zarephath (1 Kings 17:14)—"the jar of flour will not be used up and the jug of oil will not run dry"—applies to all us small-plate girls, too.

The Holy Spirit has been teaching me vital lessons about having an itty-bitty plate with turkey platter-sized desires. First, I've realized that if God had given me a large enough capacity to match my oversized dreams, my arrogance would know no bounds. I'd be unbearably proud of *my* amazing abilities, giving myself all the glory. Instead, I am keenly aware that God is constantly multiplying my meager offerings. I watch in constant wonder as things happen that I'm aware I'm not doing by myself.

Second, I'm learning to accept help and regularly ask for it. No more waiting until I'm desperate for rescue (which makes me feel so ashamed I swear I'll never need anyone ever again). No more trying to prove I can do it all. Instead, I'm getting better at doing the few things God has called me to do and collaboratively serving with other women who are doing exactly what God has called them to do too.

IT'S AN AMAZING GIFT TO BE A SMALL PART OF HUGE
MIRACLES. AND ALL THE CREDIT GOES TO HIM.

Best of all, I now know that it's never a mistake when God pairs an itty-bitty saucer with enormous dreams. It's an amazing gift to be a small part of huge miracles. And all the credit goes to him.

Download a printable of the six-word prayer at
www.SensitiveAndStrongBook.com

The Gift of Service

Finding Your Place in a Hurting World

Denise

Years ago, I sat in a stadium with thousands of other women. We were there to hear from some of our favorite speakers and be encouraged in the Word. At one point, a large organization spent 20 minutes or so sharing about their work around the world in the hopes of garnering financial support for their mission.

That's when I saw the video—a reenactment of a true story. A very poor, uneducated family in a far-flung village entrusted their pre-adolescent girl to a passerby who promised to provide an education and a good home for her. The promises, of course, were never realized as the young girl was horrifically abused and trafficked.

I sat there dumbfounded at the shock of it all. I knew all too well about abuse, but I thought it happened in individual and isolated instances. I had no idea it was a *business*—a well-organized and sophisticated industry, affecting millions around the world. So, I did what I normally do whenever I hear about tragedy and heartache: My empathy shifted into high gear. In my mind, I entered that locked room with the nameless girl. I entered her pain, and I stared at the bolted door, desperately wishing someone would come and set me free.

Being an HSP means our empathy can go into overdrive. We don't just hear about something tragic and try to process it intellectually, we enter into it with our hearts and our minds and we imagine what it would be like to be in that situation, and the weight of it can be overwhelming.

Surrounded by thousands of well-dressed, presumably middle-class women, I felt helpless. What can one person do? Can writing a check each month really put a dent in the enormity of this problem? I began to pray that somehow God would open a way for me to take an active part, however small, in rescuing and restoring victims of trafficking.

When Empathy Becomes a Catalyst for Change

With the advent of the Internet, we now have the ability to hear about tragedies happening everywhere, even in remote parts of the country or faraway corners of the earth. Hearing about heartache is no longer confined to our own local community and the nightly six o'clock news. If you scroll through your social media feed for five minutes, you'll likely encounter yet another tale of sorrow from somewhere in the world.

Sometimes it's more than my HSP heart can take. When sorrow strikes, I want to be there for my friends and family; I want to come alongside members of my church and local community. But one person cannot take on the sorrows of the entire world. Only God is strong enough for that. The needs of the world far exceed our limited resources and abilities, but that doesn't mean we can close our eyes to a hurting world. Every one of us can do something. Even HSPs.

> OUR TRUE IDENTITY IN LIFE IS NOT FOUND IN
> BEING AN HSP; RATHER, OUR IDENTITY
> IS FOUND IN CHRIST ALONE.

We must remember that our true identity in life is not found in being an HSP; rather, our identity is found in Christ alone, and as believers, we have the Holy Spirit living inside us. Scripture reminds us that "the Spirit God gave us does not make us timid, but gives us power, love and self-discipline" (2 Timothy 1:7). We are not mere sensitives. We have a spirit of power dwelling inside us, and by God's grace and power, we can become catalysts for change. And our empathy can point us to where we might best be able to serve.

HSPs are deeply sensitive to the wounds of others. We can easily take on someone else's pain as our own, but rather than grow overwhelmed by the sheer number of needs around us, we can prayerfully ask God where he would like us to serve. Where we serve and the way we serve will look different for each of us, but every single one of us is part of what the Apostle Peter calls "the priesthood." In 1 Peter 2:9, Peter writes, "But you are a chosen people, a royal priesthood, a holy nation, God's special possession, that you may declare the praises of him who called you out of darkness into his wonderful light." For many of us, the ministry we are called to will have something to do with the darkness from which we have been delivered.

> WHERE DOES YOUR DEEPEST PASSION INTERSECT
> WITH THE WORLD'S DEEPEST PAIN?

Pastor Rick Warren of Saddleback Church has been quoted saying, "Your greatest ministry will come out of your deepest hurt."[1] Where have you experienced Christ's freedom? Chances are good that you'll be called to bring Christ's light to others who are in the same darkness you once experienced. Frederick Buechner puts it another way, saying, "The place God calls you to is the place where your deep gladness and the world's deep hunger meet."[2] In other words, where does your deepest passion intersect with the world's deepest pain?

What Jesus Can Do with Your Story

We can comfort others with the same comfort we have received from God (2 Corinthians 1:4). If you have endured the effects of chemotherapy and radiation, you can come alongside those who are still reeling from a scary diagnosis and are unsure of what the future holds. If you have walked the painful road of divorce, you can walk beside a friend who has found herself on the same road. If you have been set free from an eating disorder, you can minister to someone who is going through a similar ordeal. If you have experienced freedom from an addiction, you can mentor someone who is feeling unsteady in her own newfound sobriety. If you have struggled with depression, you can speak hope into the heart of someone feeling the weight of depression right now.

For me, I can come alongside victims of sexual abuse and testify to the healing that comes through Christ. I have known what it is like to be a child, completely outsized and overpowered by the only other person in the room, wishing someone would walk through the door and rescue me. When I first heard about human trafficking, it affected me deeply in part because I'm sensitive to stories of suffering, but also in part because I, too, am a survivor of abuse. My story is different, though, from many of the stories I have heard over the years, because when I finally told my parents what had happened at a neighbor's house, they called the police. An arrest was made. A trial was held. A sentence was given. And jail time was served.

I can remember sitting in my bedroom with a female police officer. She sat across from me on a kid-sized chair, wearing her navy uniform. A black baton dangled from her belt and clanked against the side of my kid-sized table. With every question she asked, I moved the head of my stuffed bear up-and-down for "yes" and side-to-side for "no." I thought that made my yeses and noes plenty clear, but the officer said I had to speak my answers. Apparently, the direction I moved my stuffed bear's head was not admissible in court. I didn't know what that meant. I just knew I hated mumbling the words.

Something about speaking the words made it more real, and I wanted it to be unreal, like a bad dream I wanted to forget. But the officer wouldn't let me. She kept asking questions and writing words on her notepad—words I couldn't see. Back then there was no such thing as #metoo. Only me. Me and a very dark secret thing for which I did not have words.

Today, women across America are speaking. With a mere five letters, women are piercing the silence of undeserved shame. Those of us who utter the five letters of #metoo are members of a sisterhood we never asked to be a part. But this is not the totality of our story. We are more than the sum of one moment, one episode, or even a series of episodes.

As long as we are breathing, our story is not over yet. There is more story to write, and I intend on writing a better story than the script I was handed when I was young. It starts with another five letters: J-e-s-u-s. For some, that may sound trite or silly or absurd, but they are the only five letters that will ever succeed in writing a new story. Just look at all the stories about Jesus. Every woman he met—the used, the abused, the forgotten, the cast-aside—they moved *toward* him.

The Samaritan woman ran to her village and invited everyone to come back to the well, *toward* the man who had just engaged her in a deeply vulnerable and profoundly theological conversation. The Canaanite mother with a gravely ill daughter endured the derision of the disciples to move *toward* Jesus. The Hebrew woman with the issue of blood was considered "unclean" according to Mosaic law and she wasn't supposed to touch anybody, but she pushed through the crowd *toward* Jesus to touch the hem of his garment. And Mary Magdalene, who had been forgiven and cleansed of so much, rushed *toward* the tomb to anoint the dead body of the man who died for her, only to turn around and become the first person to tell the world of the risen Lord.

Jesus was likely the first man these women ever met who made them truly feel safe, the first man who looked into their eyes with deep compassion, without a trace of anything resembling a threat.

I've met him, too, in the pages of the greatest story ever told. Perhaps it's ironic—the justice poetic—that what one man stole another man restored. Since then, I've spent untold hours in the classroom as a teacher, and there's just this knowing. When a young woman has been abused, I can see it in her eyes, her body language. First one, then another. I've been the one she came to with her secret, the one she trusted to help her hope again.

My ministry may look different than your ministry, but we can all minister to one other with the hope we have found in Christ. I can say #metoo, but then I add to that the greatest truth of all: Because of Jesus, I've been set free.

Set free from the lie that my story was ruined. *It wasn't!*
Set free from the fear that no man can be trusted. *Many can!*
Set free from the worry that true intimacy is not possible. *It is!*

Because of Christ's healing grace, my #metoo story has become a look-at-what-Jesus-can-do story! What has Jesus done in your life? What is your story? That very well may be the place God wants to use you in his kingdom.

Your Passion and the World's Pain

For many years, I have shared my story with women in one-on-one settings. I have never shared it from a microphone, but I have tried to be faithful whenever the Lord brought someone across my path who needed to hear hope and grace and truth. Then, last year I was invited to join the board of directors of a faith-based nonprofit organization that serves women rescued from human trafficking. That prayer I prayed all those years ago? God heard it, and in his providential timing, he opened a door for me to serve.

As HSPs, our empathy can become a catalyst for change. We don't need to be overwhelmed by the size of the need. We don't need to be overcome by a flood of emotion. We just need to find where we're called to serve. Let's invite God to lead us to the ministry he's been preparing us for all along. Let's look to Jesus and the new story he has written over us. And let's listen to the guidance of the Holy Spirit.

What is most important is this: To paraphrase Buechner, wherever your heart's deepest passion meets the world's greatest pain, that is likely the place where you're being called to serve. That is where you can turn your empathy into action for change.

20

The Gift of Listening

Becoming the Best Kind of Friend

Denise

When I think of the women who have made the greatest impact on my life, I notice they all have one thing in common: They're really good listeners.

As a child, I practically grew up at my grandma's house. She would set the tea kettle on the stove, pull out her favorite teacups, and open a fresh package of Lorna Doone shortbread cookies. Because nothing says "I love you" like Lorna Doones and a long session of listening. Grandma loved to listen; she truly seemed to savor every word. As a teen, I loved hanging out with my youth pastor's wife, too. I used to drive to her house and hang out with her while her firstborn played on the floor between us. I would tell her everything happening at school, and she showed genuine interest in the details of a teenager's life.

> THE WOMEN WHO HAVE MADE THE GREATEST IMPACT ON MY LIFE ALL HAVE ONE THING IN COMMON: THEY'RE REALLY GOOD LISTENERS.

I do not know if my grandma or my youth pastor's wife were HSPs (although I have my suspicions), but I do know they gave me the gift of listening. Whenever I was with them, I felt seen, heard, and loved.

Today, the art of listening is harder to come by. Between social media sites and the ease of instant messaging, the world around us has only gotten noisier as it seems everyone is talking, talking, talking. The once-quiet cafés I used to frequent have now mounted large-screen TVs on the walls, and most of the patrons have a smartphone next to their fork and spoon. We can hardly go half an hour without someone on a screen talking at us.

You could say we're "listening" all the time, but when the person we are listening to is on the other side of a screen, our listening becomes more passive than we may realize. Active listening—especially when a person is directly in front of you—is a much different thing. True listening takes intention and concentration, and it's one of the greatest gifts we can give another human being.

The Gift of Listening

In the last chapter, we talked about how to respond when we hear stories of great suffering and how to minister to others with the same comfort we have received from God. But what can we do when our friends and loved ones are going through painful circumstances with which we have no experience whatsoever? How can we be a good friend to those who are walking through a season of heartbreak when we feel utterly helpless and do not know how to respond?

In these situations, we can give the gift of being near and listening well. To be a good listener doesn't require firsthand experience of what someone else is going through. It simply requires that we show up with a heart ready to listen.

Dr. Elaine Aron says that "HSPs have a gift for listening and understanding."[1] This makes sense when you consider the things that make HSPs unique. We notice nuance and pick up on subtleties. And when you add these strengths to a heart easily swamped with empathy, HSPs have all the makings of being a good listener. But it's not a given. Just like our non-HSP friends, HSPs must cultivate the skills of being a good listener, and when these skills are compounded with the natural strengths of an HSP, a beautiful gift can emerge.

The Art of Listening Well

How can HSPs grow in the area of listening well? How can we take our natural tendencies as HSPs and become really good listeners? How can we give the gift of listening to those we love, and even those we've just met?

We have all been guilty of "not hearing" someone who is in the same room as us. Perhaps we were busy cooking dinner or preoccupied with feeding the dog or distracted with a new message on our phones. Thankfully, we can become better listeners with greater intention.

First, to grow as a listener requires listening to the Holy Spirit. As the Spirit guides us, we are better able to serve those around us. How can we know it's really the Spirit guiding us and not our own intuition? The more time we spend reading God's Word, the more easily we will recognize his voice when he speaks. God is steadfast, which means he speaks with consistency. The better we know God, the better we know his voice.

Second, being a good listener requires an attitude of selflessness. It means placing someone else's needs above our own. It means doing what the Apostle Paul says in Philippians 2:4 and looking not only to our own interests, but also to the interests of others. Listening well necessitates selflessness, and selflessness is an attitude of the heart that must be learned by everybody, including HSPs.

To consider other people's needs above our own doesn't come naturally to anybody. As believers in Christ, we understand that we were born with a sinful nature. What is a toddler's favorite first word? *Mine.* Thinking about ourselves is automatic. How many times have I been in a conversation where I spent most of the time half-listening while simultaneously preparing in my mind what I would say next? By God's grace, however, we can grow in humility and adopt a heart attitude of otherness. None of the following tips on listening well will mean much if we do not intentionally place the other person's needs in front of our own—at least for the time being.

Once our hearts are in a posture of being others-focused, we can do the following:

- Pray for God to open your heart to really hear what needs to be heard.

- Listen with your body language. Lean in. Unfold your arms. Make eye contact. Nod occasionally.

- Refuse the temptation to interrupt. Let the other person have the floor.

- Restate what you have heard to make sure you have heard everything correctly.

- Refrain from offering advice or solutions. Just listen.

- Ask occasional questions for clarification.

- Do not minimize the weight of what the other person is feeling.

- Avoid responding with your own similar tale.

- Remember that this is not about you.

Above all, keep in mind that even as you give the gift of listening, the other person is also giving you a gift. As she shares a personal story with you, she is entrusting you with a vulnerable place in her heart. To receive what another person is sharing forms a sacred bond of trust.

The Greatest Listener of All

To listen is an act of love. Listening is how we say to another person, "I'm here because I care. What you're going through is important to me, and what is happening inside of you is important, too. I am here to hear you because I am here for you."

The One who has modeled this best for us is the One who has made us. We cannot talk about becoming a great listener without recognizing the greatest listener of all. Scripture says we love because God first loved us (1 John 4:19). That also means we listen because he first listened to us.

We serve a God who listens! Psalm 18:6 says, "In my distress I called upon the LORD; to my God I cried for help. From his temple he heard my voice, and my cry to him reached his ears" (ESV). When we cry out to God, he hears us. More than that, he responds to our cries. Psalm

116:1-2 says, "I love the LORD, because he has heard my voice and my pleas for mercy. Because he inclined his ear to me, therefore I will call on him as long as I live" (ESV). The God who made the stars with the merest whisper of his voice is the same God who inclines his ear to us. What lavish listening grace he bestows upon us!

A Beautiful Tradition

How can we share this listening grace with those who have experienced a crushing loss, like the loss of a loved one? Whether we have personally experienced such a loss or not, we can still be there for those who are wading through waves of grief.

There's a beautiful Jewish custom called "sitting shiva" that fosters true listening. In Hebrew, the word *shiva* means *seven*. Sitting shiva occurs in the seven days that follow the burial of a loved one. During those seven days, visitors can come and sit with those who are mourning, and certain rules of etiquette must be observed. Upon entering the home of those who are mourning, the visitor does not know whether the person mourning wants to retell fond memories of the deceased or have a moment's respite and talk about the weather, so the visitor remains silent and lets the mourner speak first. The job of the visitor is to listen. Whatever the mourner talks about is what the visitor will talk about.

This is a beautiful act of listening and following another person's lead. We can all do this. When someone we care about is hurting, one of the best ways we can be a good friend is by being a good listener.

The Listeners Among Us

One of my favorite listeners in the Bible is Luke. His gospel account is the longest of the four records of the life, death, and resurrection of Jesus. What's interesting about Luke is the fact that he wasn't an eyewitness—not like Matthew and John. While Mark likely penned the first-person stories of Peter, who was also an eyewitness, Luke went about the business of a historian. Luke opens his book by saying:

> Many have undertaken to draw up an account of the things
> that have been fulfilled among us, just as they were handed

down to us by those who from the first were eyewitnesses
and servants of the word. With this in mind, since I myself
have carefully investigated everything from the beginning,
I too decided to write an orderly account for you, most
excellent Theophilus (Luke 1:1-3).

How did Luke "carefully investigate" the life of Jesus and the events
of the early church? There was no such thing as Google back then, and
no such thing as a set of A-to-Z encyclopedias either. An investigation
in Luke's day required interviewing eyewitnesses. Luke had to be an
excellent listener in order to write an accurate historical account.

Only in the Gospel of Luke do we have the privilege of hearing
Mary's story of how she visited her cousin Elizabeth when she became
pregnant. Only Luke records the "Magnificat"—Mary's song of praise.
Only Luke tells us how Mary pondered in her heart all the things surrounding Jesus's birth. How did Luke learn these details? He likely
interviewed Mary.[2] He listened with a quill in hand as Mary told the
greatest story of all time.

Today, one of my favorite listeners is a dear woman named Debby,
a retired nurse. Every week our church hosts a Wednesday night
AWANAS program. The kids are supposed to come and recite a memory verse, but some of them get nervous speaking in front of the whole
room, so Debby walks to each classroom, and one by one, the kids can
step into the hallway and recite their Bible verse to Debby. She listens.
If they don't have a Bible verse memorized, they can simply tell Debby
about their week. And she listens.

> TO LISTEN WELL IS TO LOVE WELL.

I think being a listener is one of the most beautiful things we can do
for others. Like Debby, you, too, can be a listener. When your friend's
husband loses his job, you can listen. When your neighbor is missing
her spouse who passed away last year, you can listen. When your girl-
friend is struggling with a bad breakup, you can listen. When your
child is working through a problem at school, you can listen.

As an HSP, you're probably already noticing the heaviness others seem to be carrying, so take the next step and ask them how they're doing—how they're *really* doing. You might not be able to solve their every problem, but chances are good that they don't want you to solve their problems anyway. They likely just want someone to listen. That's something you can do with grace and a gentle ear.

We all long to be heard. We long to be known. We long to be accepted. That is the beautiful gift God has given to us, and it's the same gift we can give to others. To listen well is to love well, and HSPs are ideally suited to give the gift of listening to those around them.

21

The Gift of Hospitality
Serving Others in the Simplest Ways

Cheri

"Isss okay, Mama! Isss okay!" Annemarie toddles into the kitchen and pats me on the shoulder. In just 20 minutes, a dozen or so guests will arrive for her second birthday party. I should be changing into a clean sweater, not sitting on the kitchen floor sobbing. But I can't help it.

I worked like a madwoman all last night and this morning, but I have so little to show for my efforts. Only half of the vegetables are washed, drained, and sliced for the appetizer tray. The *Beauty and the Beast* party decorations are still in the Michael's bag. I need to clean the guest bathroom and vacuum at least the family room and living room. My husband, Daniel, is on his way to the store to pick up the drinks and ice that I forgot last night. And the cake...the cake is the reason the little birthday girl keeps assuring me, "Isss okay, Mama! Isss okay!"

Except it's not okay. It's a disaster. I'm an experienced cake decorator. But the project I thought would take 30 minutes has stretched beyond three hours, and it's still not done. My hands are cramped from squeezing tiny frosting stars, one-by-one, all over a cake that was supposed to end up looking exactly like Belle...not an alien.

The doorbell rings. I haul myself off the floor, mop my face with a handful of Kleenexes, and brace myself for hours of playing a role that exhausts and overwhelms me: hostess.

When It's Hard to be an HSP Hostess

My mother was the ultimate "hostess with the mostest." When she entertained, she planned her meal not just with recipe cards, but colored sketches of the filled dinner plates to guarantee an attractive array of colors. When she said, "lunch will be served at 1:00 p.m.," lunch was served at 1:00 p.m., give or take ten seconds. Hot foods hot, cold foods cold. She appeared to pull it off effortlessly, never breaking a sweat or allowing anyone in the kitchen to help.

In stark contrast, I spent decades serving monochromatic meals, an hour (or two) late, hot foods tepid, and me mere moments from a meltdown. My every attempt to reproduce my mother's skill in the kitchen felt like a dismal disaster. By the time my guests arrived, the last thing I wanted to do was eat or attempt conversation. All I wanted to do was hide in my bedroom until they left!

Reading Scripture admonishing me to "offer hospitality to one another without grumbling" (1 Peter 4:9) only made me feel guiltier and more ashamed. I constantly berated myself: *What's wrong with me? Why can't I do something as simple as preparing and serving a meal for a few guests? It's not that hard!* It was Denise who answered both of these questions for me, connecting the dots from feeling overwhelmed by hospitality to being an HSP. She explained:

> When I learned about being an HSP, all of a sudden it made so much sense why I hate to cook. It's such a multi-sensory process. There's so much all at once. The chopping and the stirring and the whipping and the kneading. The smelling of all the aromas and, of course, all the tasting along the way. There's the buzzing of the timer going off, the clicking of the gas stove, and the bubbling of the boiling water. And you're usually running dishes in the dishwasher simultaneously because there are so many dirty dishes when you cook. Cooking means constant sensory stimuli, so by the time I'm finished, I'm so exhausted I can't even enjoy the meal.

As I listened to Denise, my aversion to all the chaos I associate with the kitchen suddenly made sense. The high-intensity meal preparation that comes so easily for a natural non-HSP hostess like my mother can be completely overwhelming for HSPs like Denise and me. Despite our best intentions—*This time, everything will go smoothly!*—preparing for guests can send us into sensory (and sometimes emotional) overload without us realizing how quickly or completely it's come over us. (Add a pinch or two of perfectionism to the mix, and you've got a real recipe for disaster.)

Six Sanity-Saving Steps for the HSP Hostess

For those of us who get caught up in kitchen chaos when we're trying to practice hospitality, here are six intentional steps we can take to create calm in the kitchen.

> THERE ARE STEPS HSPs CAN TAKE TO
> CREATE CALM IN THE KITCHEN.

1. Take breaks.

It may feel counterintuitive to think about taking breaks before you've gotten started, but intermittent breaks are vital when chaos starts creeping in. Breaks aren't a luxury, something we'll do if there's time. They're a necessity. Taking a break simply means getting out of the kitchen for a few minutes to:

- Pray for your guests, for your family, for your own heart.
- Sit in a favorite chair with a good book.
- Recline on the couch (with or without a purring cat!).
- Write in a gratitude journal.
- Listen to quiet (or upbeat) music.
- Take a brisk walk.
- And whatever else might work for you!

The goal of the break is a change of state. Think of it as "cleansing the palate" of your head and heart before you move on to the next stage of meal preparation.

2. Make a written plan.

I used to trust my intuition to tell me when to start preparing my various recipes and which order to put them in the oven. But I always ended up with some dishes done an hour too early and others a full hour away from being ready. Now, I employ backwards design. I figure out how long each dish needs to bake, cook, set, or chill. Then I do the math to calculate when I need to begin, factoring in my breaks.

When I first started making a written plan, I was shocked—*It can't possibly take that long!* And even embarrassed—*I should figure out ways to shave time off that total.* Such calculations, however, are far more realistic than gut feels or guilt-filled "shoulds" will ever be. Instead of berating ourselves, we can assure ourselves—*It takes as much time as it takes.*

3. Prepare ahead.

Back when I dreaded hospitality, I procrastinated everything until the last possible moment. This caused a ton of kitchen chaos, which kept the whole self-reinforcing cycle spinning. Now, part of my written plan includes figuring out everything I can do ahead of time. Like the house cleaning. I used to try to whip my house into shape on the same day I was doing all the cooking. Talk about sensory overload! Not to mention going all day without a single break. No wonder I was a wreck when guests arrived. Now, I schedule all deep-cleaning for the days prior and do strategic touch-ups (and, if you have young children, selective giving-ups) on the day of. Preparing in advance includes:

- buying premade ingredients rather than making everything homemade
- doing the chopping, slicing, and dicing a day or two ahead
- taking the first step of a recipe (such as cooking the rice for a casserole) the night before

Fixing a meal feels so much less daunting when everything is ready to "throw and go"!

4. Accept help.

I used to mimic my mother's habit of shooing everyone out of the kitchen. Partly because I didn't want to admit I needed help, but mostly because I was flying by the seat of my pants so badly, I couldn't even articulate the help I needed. Now, when someone says, "How can I help?" I refer to my plan and give them a specific answer. It's a reciprocal gift when we're prepared to say:

- "Could you peel and slice the carrots? Everything you need is laid out here."
- "Would you put those rolls in that basket and cover them with one of these napkins?"
- "If you could pour the drink—it's on the top shelf of the fridge—that would be wonderful!"

5. Clean as you go.

This is one of my mother's habits I've embraced as my own. Before each break, I quickly scrub and rinse everything in the sink and set the dishes in the drainer to air dry. When I return, I use a towel as necessary and put things back where they belong. For some, this might feel like adding extra work in the middle. Why not save the clean-up to the very end and do it all at once? But for others, pausing to tame the chaos is a smart step toward sanity. Starting the next stage of meal preparation in a clean kitchen can create a sense of calm.

6. Have Option B...and C (and possibly even D).

"Everything must turn out perfectly because I have no back-up plan if anything fails" is way too much pressure to put on yourself. Not to mention the other people in your home. Hope for the best, and plan for the worst. In a worst-case scenario, I keep a stash of non-perishable ingredients on hand for a full meal that's quick to pull together. I also keep a few gift cards to local restaurants in case I need to make a last-minute call for delivery.

"Hospitality means inviting people into my home" is a narrow definition that also puts unnecessary pressure on you. What about collaborating with a friend to cohost a special meal with you—at her home? Or gathering a group for fellowship at a local coffee shop? Or combining forces at a non-home location, such as a church fellowship hall, to cook, chat, and clean together?

A Do-Over Story

"Cheri, could you and Daniel host our guest speaker for lunch today?" our principal texts me. "He was planning to come to our house, but we've got a family emergency on our hands."

Years ago, a request like this would have produced abject panic. But today I simply smile and type back, "Of course! It will be simple: soups and sandwiches. We've already got a group of students coming over, and he's welcome to join us."

I lay out another place setting on the table, then stir the store-bought soups that are warming in several small Crock-Pots. After putting my famous homemade rolls in the oven to bake for 15 minutes, I relax on the couch and listen to a favorite podcast until the timer buzzes. Once the rolls are cooling on a rack, I touch up the guest bathroom and run a Swiffer across the downstairs hardwood floors.

> THE REASON WE'RE CALLED TO PRACTICE HOSPITALITY ISN'T TO SHOW OFF A PERFECTLY CLEAN HOME OR SERVE UP PERFECTLY PREPARED FOOD; IT'S TO WELCOME AND SERVE OTHERS.

A student walks in the front door without bothering to knock. "Mrs. G, it's me! I came early to help." Glancing at my written plan to see what needs to be done next, I respond, "Hey, Michael! Can you get the strawberries out of the fridge, rinse them, and slice them for dessert? You'll find a big bowl in the cupboard to the left of the sink."

Half an hour later, as I'm loading the dishwasher, the doorbell rings. I pause to remind myself that the reason we're called to "practice hospitality" (Romans 12:13) isn't to show off a perfectly clean home or serve up perfectly prepared food; it's to welcome and serve others. Smiling in anticipation of the reciprocal blessings God has in store, I open the door and step into a role I'm learning to enjoy: hostess.

You'll find a printable Backwards Design Meal Planning Guide at www.SensitiveAndStrongBook.com.

The Gift of Creativity
Blessing Others with Your God-Given Talents

Denise

When I was young, I did not think of myself as a particularly creative person. In art class, we had to draw and paint and sometimes sculpt objects with modeling clay, but my creations never turned out quite right. One time, my art teacher instructed everyone to take off a shoe, place it on our desks, and draw a replication of it. The finished picture of my Reebok tennis shoe looked more like a flat tire with strings. Because I couldn't draw a stick figure to save my life, I assumed my failures as a drawer, painter, and sculptor meant I was not endowed with any talent in the creativity department.

Thankfully, there's more to creativity than pictures or sculptures. In high school, I had a teacher entrust me with a giant bulletin board in her classroom. The upcoming holiday provided the broader theme, but I could create any scene I wanted with the craft materials my teacher gave me. I discovered I had a knack for telling stories on bulletin boards with little more than paper, markers, glue, and scissors. Over time, I continued to create stories with words on paper, and I learned that coloring pencils and paints are not my instruments of choice. I prefer a blank page with a simple black ink pen over a blank canvas with a palette of colors. My imagination can take it from there.

If you've ever said you are not a creative person, or you've adamantly declared that creativity is not your thing, it is possible that you're making these declarations based on a narrow definition of art. Most of us think of art as something stemming from a middle school art class where we were forced to try our hand at drawing or painting and the results turned out embarrassingly bad. But creativity is more than making a final product that someone else might deem to be "art."

Creativity can take on many forms. It may involve taking raw materials and refashioning them in such a way that something new is formed out of them—like baking and cooking, sewing and quilting, gardening and landscaping. Or it may involve using abstract ideas and shaping them in such a way that something cohesive emerges—like writing and storytelling, ideating and problem solving, composing and arranging music. The outlets for creativity are endless.

Connecting the Dots with Creativity

Many books and articles have linked creativity with Sensory Processing Sensitivity.[1] This makes sense when you think about the amount of data an HSP absorbs every hour of every day. What does an HSP do with all that data? Imagine each incremental piece of data as a simple dot. An HSP takes in a lot of "dots" throughout the day and then works overtime to process all those "dots" into some form of cohesive meaning. Creativity occurs when we connect the dots and construct meaning from the information we have gleaned. This often happens in the form of new insights or ideas.

In their book *Wired to Create: Unraveling the Mysteries of the Creative Mind*, Scott Barry Kaufman and Carolyn Gregoire say, "If we think of creativity as 'connecting the dots' in some way, then sensitive people experience a world in which there are both more dots and more opportunities for connection."[2] Connecting the dots can look like planning an event and bringing together different elements that emphasize the event's theme. Maybe you invite someone to share their story that is a great example of the event's theme. Perhaps you put together table centerpieces that reflect the theme. Maybe you create a printed program that ties the theme together beautifully. Or maybe you bring together a group of people who contribute their own unique gifts to the event. Maybe you have a talent for connecting talented people!

> FOR MANY HSPs, CREATIVITY IS AN EXTERNAL EXPRESSION OF THEIR INTERNAL COMMOTION.

What are some ways you "connect the dots"? For many HSPs, creativity is an external expression of their internal commotion. Deborah Ward at *Psychology Today* says that for HSPs creativity is "the pressure valve for all that accumulated emotional and sensory data."[3] In other words, creativity is an outlet for all that input! For me, writing is the way I exhale. I process my thoughts and sort my feelings with ink on paper. For you, it might be something else, but our creativity can be more than personal, therapeutic catharsis. We can use our creativity as a means to bless others.

To Create and Bless

Which materials do you most enjoy working with? Here are some ideas for blessing others with your creativity.

If you enjoy working with fabrics, perhaps you could:

- Knit tiny hats for premature infants.
- Crochet soft blankets for patients in children's hospitals.
- Make a quilt for a friend going through a difficult season.
- Create other simple gifts, like coasters or aprons, to tell a friend you're thinking about them.

If you enjoy working with wood, perhaps you could:

- Build a desk for a small child.
- Create a jewelry box for a widow on your street.
- Build a table and chairs for a family in need.

- Make a Pinewood Derby racetrack for your local Cub Scouts.

If you enjoy working with foods, perhaps you could:

- Make a meal for a friend who just had surgery.
- Bake a special dessert for your pastor and his family.
- Offer to teach college students how to cook the basics.
- Share some of your favorite recipes with friends online.

If you enjoy working with ideas, perhaps you could:

- Join a church committee to help brainstorm solutions for a specific challenge.
- Think of analogies that help explain difficult-to-understand concepts.
- Write a story that inspires and share it with readers online.

If you enjoy working with paper, perhaps you could:

- Volunteer to wrap presents for busy working moms.
- Create personalized stationery for someone who is unable to leave their home.
- Learn hand-lettering and design Christmas cards for friends.

If you enjoy working with photography, perhaps you could:

- Put together a 12-month calendar with your favorite photos and give to friends.
- Inspire friends on social media with photos of nature and beauty.
- Offer to teach a class on photography.

If you enjoy working with words, perhaps you could:

- Send a friend a list of words that best describe her: caring, generous, funny, etc.

- Handwrite a *thank you* note to someone you noticed doing something kind.

- Start a book club and encourage life-giving discussions on great literature.

Creativity can be so much more than drawing or painting a picture. The possibilities are endless.

The creative process might begin as something deeply personal. It might start out as a way to express something you are experiencing deep inside, but your creativity can become a beautiful means of blessing others, too. Dolly Parton has been quoted saying, "I'm a very sensitive person. I hurt real easy and real deep, which is why I think I have to write songs, [and] why so many of them fit the feelings of so many people that can't write. It's because I feel everything to my core."[4] What Dolly Parton describes is exactly what Oswald Chambers explains in his classic devotional *My Utmost for His Highest*:

> If you cannot express yourself on any subject, struggle until you can. If you do not, someone will be the poorer all the days of his life. Struggle to reexpress some truth of God to yourself, and God will use that expression to someone else. Go through the winepress of God where the grapes are crushed. You must struggle to get expression experimentally, then there will come a time when that expression will become the very wine of strengthening to someone else.[5]

Perhaps your song or your story or your poem will help someone else find the expression they've been looking for. Perhaps your creativity will be the gift someone needed in that very moment.

One of the Sweetest Blessings I Ever Received

When I was pregnant with my first child, I received a quilt from a friend who was in her early twenties like me. With various pastel fabrics, the quilt had a rocking horse pattern on the front, which was the nursery theme I had chosen. It wasn't the kind of gift you could find in a store anywhere, so I asked my friend, "Did you make this?"

She smiled and nodded.

I was so taken aback by her generosity, I stammered, "How did you learn to make quilts?"

She said, "Well, I didn't know how, but my mom has made lots of quilts over the years, so I asked her to teach me how to make a quilt because I wanted to give you one."

The custom baby quilt in my hands was so much more than a blanket. It represented hours and hours of love, just for me and my baby. Every time I looked at it, I thought of a mom teaching her 20-something daughter how to cut pieces and stitch appliques. I thought of my friend learning how to do something new, so she could give me a special gift.

Her gift inspired me to learn how to quilt because I knew right away that someday I would want to teach my baby girl how to make quilts, too. Thirteen years later, that dream of mine came true. When my daughter's great-grandmother was about to have her eightieth birthday celebration, I let my daughter pick out the pattern of her choice. She selected one with large colorful flowers on a white background, and she picked out all the fabrics. Stitch by stitch, I showed her how to lay the pieces and sew them together. When it was finished, she had a very special gift to give her great-grandma.

> WHICHEVER WAY YOU TURN YOUR SENSITIVITY INTO A BEAUTIFUL OUTWARD EXPRESSION, THAT CAN BE YOUR GIFT TO OTHERS.

Maybe quilting isn't your thing. That's okay. Whichever way you turn your sensitivity into a beautiful outward expression, that can be your gift to others. And maybe your gift is just the thing this hurting world needs.

The Gift of Influence

Leveraging Your Unique Strengths for Leadership

Cheri

I haven't even eaten breakfast yet, but I'm already filled with self-doubt. Although the cover of the shiny new binder I've just been handed says "Welcome to the Leadership Program Orientation," the inner critic in my head demands: *Who do you think you are? What on earth are you doing here? These people already know each other. You don't belong. Do you really think you have what it takes to be a leader?*

I respond to the last question the way I have for decades: *No, I know I'm not a real leader. I'm not made of leadership material. I don't have what it takes.* Yet, I force myself to participate in the group activity I'm supposed to be doing with my new Leadership and Learning Group. We need to create a structure that represents our leadership styles using random pieces of PVC piping. I'm one of two newbies to the group. Harold, clearly an extrovert, dives into action without the slightest hesitation. Although I'm also an extrovert, I hang back, observing, listening, assessing the setting, the task, and the people...because that's what HSPs do.

How am I supposed to figure out what represents "us" when I've just met these people?

The other eight group members have been in the program for years, so they collaborate with the ease of people who have taken classes, shared meals, and prayed together time and time again. Their easy banter and inside jokes make me feel like I'm fading into the distance, perhaps disappearing altogether.

"What are you doing?"

I'm so lost in thought that Harold's question startles me. My mind blank, I stare and gape like a fish thrown on dry land by a sudden wave. Finally, I blurt out, "I'm watching."

"What kind of leader does *that*?" he snaps back.

His question silences me, confirming my worst fears: *I'm not a real leader. I'm not made of leadership material. I don't have what it takes.*

Leadership and HSPs

I've always imagined that a real leader:

- exudes confidence and self-assurance
- effortlessly moves audiences to laughter and tears
- speaks off the cuff, straight from the heart, all impromptu with no preparation, no notes
- looks the part, from clothing to hairstyle to accessories (which include car, spouse, kids, pets, etc.)
- makes incisive snap judgments and instant decisions
- casts an inspiring vision for the future
- motivates everyone around them to enthusiastically join their cause
- is larger than life, a "force of nature"
- commands attention and respect just by walking into the room
- decimates opponents with ready rhetoric and sharp wit
- thrives on sudden changes and new challenges
- is always in control, of themselves and others

When we hold up our HSP qualities against this list, it's easy to feel like we pale—if not completely disappear—in comparison. We may even predisqualify ourselves from leadership opportunities, believing we don't have what it takes and that what we do have gets in the way of leading.

I didn't learn that I'm an HSP until I was almost done with my MA program, feeling drawn to pursue a PhD in Leadership. But when I described what being an HSP means to my graduate school advisor, she laughed and said, "It sounds like HPSs aren't really made of leadership material," which simultaneously hurt my feelings...*and* made me want to prove her wrong! In a synthesis paper I wrote at the end of my Leadership Theories course, I summarized my personal theory of leadership this way:

The leadership theory I am developing is a reaction against leadership "wisdom" that results in humans pushing themselves to the point that they set no boundaries, allow no margins for emergency situations, get ever-fewer hours sleep, and ultimately "crash" due to a literal accident or health incident. I am frustrated by the super-human qualities that most leadership theories prescribe; when I read the lists of inherent "traits" or "key characteristics" that appear so unattainable, I feel like I should quit the Leadership Program and resign from teaching, lest I be discovered to be a complete fraud in both arenas. In order for my personal leadership theory to work for me, it must take into account the weaknesses of my temperament, the limitations of my followers, and the restrictions of my situation. And it must help me decide not just how to lead, but also if, when, and who to lead.

A Better Way to Lead

My original beliefs about what constitutes a "real leader" were all focused on a charismatic leader—the "Mighty Likeable Fellow" that Susan Cain describes in chapter 1 of *Quiet*.[1] During my childhood, and for decades after, Charismatic Leadership was constantly held up as the ultimate style of leadership. But as the catastrophic effects of its abuses have become increasingly and repeatedly public, Charismatic Leadership has fallen from its unintended pedestal. No longer considered *the* gold standard, it has taken its place in the lineup of recognized, researched, and respected forms of influence.

While the misuse of Charismatic Leadership has been under

scrutiny, another leadership theory has been quietly gaining ground: Servant Leadership. According to Robert Greenleaf, founder of the secular theory of Servant Leadership, the best test of "success" is this:

> Do those served grow as persons? Do they, while being served, become healthier, wiser, freer, more autonomous, and are likely themselves to become servants? And what is the effect on the least privileged in society? Will they benefit, or at least not further be harmed?[2]

Of course, Servant Leadership is nothing new. It is the leadership style taught and exemplified by Jesus, the ultimate Servant Leader.

> Jesus called them together and said, "You know that those who are regarded as rulers of the Gentiles lord it over them, and their high officials exercise authority over them. Not so with you. Instead, whoever wants to become great among you must be your servant, and whoever wants to be first must be slave of all. For even the Son of Man did not come to be served, but to serve, and to give his life as a ransom for many" (Mark 10:42-45).

Take a look at the key qualities of Charismatic Leadership and Servant Leadership side by side. Notice which qualities resonate with your natural wiring, your life experience thus far, and the God-given desires that the Holy Spirit quietly stirs within your heart:

CHARISMATIC LEADER[3]	SERVANT LEADER[4]
1. Expects respect.	1. Exhibits humility.
2. Is seen as larger than life.	2. Lives authentically.
3. Accepts self.	3. Accepts others.
4. Is driven and determined.	4. Provides direction.
5. Benefits from heirarchy.	5. Engages in stewardship.
6. Focuses on results.	6. Develops and empowers people.

Servant Leadership is a universal leadership style, effective with whomever and wherever you are leading: the Bible study group at church, your own children at home, a team of colleagues in the office.

While many HSPs have felt that their sensory sensitivity automatically disqualified them from leadership, a closer look shows that the very HSP qualities that prevent us from being Charismatic leaders prequalify us as potential Servant Leaders! With training, development, and the Holy Spirit's guidance, you can learn to lead in ways that meet others' needs while stretching your comfort zone.

What It Means to Be Made of "Leadership Material"

Another area in which healthy HSPs are prewired for leadership is Emotional Intelligence. According to psychologist Daniel Goleman, author of *Emotional Intelligence: Why It Can Matter More Than IQ*:

> The most effective leaders are all alike in one crucial way: they all have a high degree of what has come to be known as emotional intelligence...My research, along with other recent studies, clearly shows that emotional intelligence is the sine qua non of leadership. Without it, a person can have the best training in the world, an incisive, analytical mind, and an endless supply of smart ideas, but...still won't make a great leader.[5]

Goleman notes that Emotional Intelligence has five key components:

1. Self-awareness
2. Self-regulation
3. Internal motivation
4. Empathy
5. Social skills

Two of these components—self-awareness and empathy—HSPs tend to have in spades. While these strengths are not unique to HSPs, they're vital aspects of leadership that we can humbly acknowledge and praise

God for. And what about the typical HSP weaknesses on this list: self-regulation and social skills? The good news you know by now is that we can intentionally strengthen these areas. In fact, your Emotional Intelligence increases as you engage in service to others.

Common HSP Leadership Concerns

> "HSPs AREN'T MADE OF
> LEADERSHIP MATERIAL" IS A LIE.

"HSPs aren't made of leadership material" is a lie. The truth is that God has gifted you with key qualities of leadership. Jesus is your role model. The Holy Spirit is your guide. And there's a hurting world that needs the sensitivity and strength of HSPs who choose to lead.

CONCERN	ACTION STEP
Conflict: As an HSP, I hate conflict. But I know leadership involves dealing with conflict. I'm concerned that my fear of conflict disqualifies me from leadership.	With training and practice, you can learn to face conflict, engage in conflict, and even initiate conflict when necessary. You may never like conflict, but you don't have to run from it either.
Empathy: My empathy makes me too gentle to be a leader. I'm concerned that I'm too soft for leadership.	Remember, your empathy also makes you caring. You can have a tender heart and also be a strong leader.
Weakness: My sensitivity has always been labeled a weakness by those I look up to. So I'm concerned that I'm too weak to be a leader.	You can use your God-given strengths to lead others while being honest about your weaknesses and choosing who you will and won't listen to. None of these are mutually exclusive.
Criticism: I'm too sensitive to criticism to be a leader. I'm concerned that I don't have thick enough skin to be a real leader.	You can develop strategies for receiving and processing criticism without developing "thick skin." (See chapter 12!)

Emotion: Leaders are logical. I'm too "touchy-feely." I'm concerned that nobody would take me seriously if I tried to lead.	None of us are all logic or all emotion. You're a blend of both. You can learn to express your "touchy-feely" nature when appropriate and dial it down as necessary. This is not all-or-nothing.
Crying: Leaders don't cry. I'm concerned that my tears automatically disqualify me from leadership.	Jesus wept. The issue isn't tears; the issue is learning to respond rather than overreact to situations. It's a skill you can practice, not something you're either born with or not.
Distance: The weight of others' needs feels too great. Leaders are able to distance themselves from individual people; I can't. I'm concerned that I don't have the objectivity necessary for leadership.	You can learn how to engage in "healthy detachment" so that you don't sink under the burden of everyone's needs. But that's not the same as distancing yourself from people as individuals. In fact, "healthy detachment" allows you to better connect with people.
Take charge: Leaders just naturally take charge; it's automatic, something they never question. I'm concerned that without a take-charge personality, I can't be a leader.	There are many styles of leadership. Some leaders "take charge" while others prefer a more collaborative approach. You can explore the options and find what works best for you and your people.
Comparison: I always feel like a fraud. Even though I care deeply about a few causes, everyone else seems so much better and smarter than me. I'm concerned that my chronic case of Imposter Syndrome means God isn't calling me to lead.	Comparison causes Imposter Syndrome. As you keep your eyes on Christ and listen to the leading of the Holy Spirit, you will become the Servant Leader God wants you to be—regardless of how much you do or do not resemble anyone else.
Snap Decisions: Leaders are quick, and take immediate action. I can deliberate on a decision for hours, days, weeks even! I'm concerned that my slow processing style is incompatible with leadership.	There's no reason to idealize snap decisions. Many leadership situations benefit from intentional reflection.

Wanted: Sensitive and Strong Leaders

During the midmorning break, as everyone else lines up for donuts and coffee, I examine the 3-D "art" my group built with PVC piping. It's long, tall on both ends, and wobbly. Rummaging through the left-over materials, I pull out one strategic piece and add it to the structure. When the other nine return and ask, "What did you do?" I point and say, "I noticed that it needed stability, so I added a bridge that connects the two ends." The others nod in understanding and approval. Now that I've added the final piece, our group structure stands solid and complete.

Harold's question echoes in my head, "What kind of leader does *that?*" and answers come to me throughout the rest of our week together: An observant leader. A reflective leader. A perceptive leader. A discerning leader. And now, many years later: a leader who is sensitive by nature and strong in the Lord.

I'm definitely not a Charismatic Leader—as a Highly Sensitive Person, I'm pretty much the exact opposite. I have no formal leadership role or fancy leadership title, and for most of my life, that was a hang-up: I believed I couldn't be a real leader without an externally-bestowed position. But according to John Maxwell, "true leadership cannot be awarded, appointed, or assigned. It comes only from influence."[6] I now know that leadership boils down to one word: *influence.*

> GOD CALLS YOU TO BE A SERVANT LEADER—TO INTENTIONALLY LISTEN TO THE HOLY SPIRIT AND FOLLOW HIS LEAD AS YOU LEAD AND SERVE OTHERS.

It was a casual comment from one of my professors that helped me finally accept that I can be both an HSP and a leader. "You lead with your words, Cheri," he said. "You influence people through your blog posts and books. You're a thought leader." To him, he was simply stating the obvious; for me, it was a redefining moment. Before our conversation, I saw myself as "just a writer." Ever since, I've recognized God's call for me to be a Servant Leader—a woman who is intentional about listening to the Holy Spirit and following his lead—through my writing and speaking.

Is there an area of your life in which you see yourself as "just a _____"? Whatever it is, although you may not have a formal leadership role or fancy leadership title, make no mistake about it: God calls you to be a Servant Leader—to intentionally listen to the Holy Spirit and follow his lead as you lead and serve others.

You'll find a list of Leadership Experience Reflection Questions, along with more Servant Leadership resources tailored to HSPs, at SensitiveAndStrongBook.com.

Epilogue

Cheri's Story

Decades ago, I read an article about what makes girls susceptible to eating disorders. Turns out that a common quality among females with food issues is a profound lack of a "sense of self." I reread the article several times, looking for a definition of "sense of self." When I couldn't find one, I spent the rest of the day trying to figure out what that phrase might mean. It finally occurred to me: If I'm struggling this much to understand what a "sense of self" is, maybe it's a sign that I haven't got one?

"So, where do I buy a new sense of self?" I wisecracked to my counselor to cover my confusion. Whose fault was my absent sense of self? Had it been stolen from me? Had I misplaced it? Or had I been born without it?

At the time, I had no idea how spot-on I was. I didn't realize how hard I'd worked to piece together my sense of self by making myself more like everybody else. I was like a telephone pole layered with posters. *Look at her gorgeous curly hair; I'll get a perm so I can have gorgeous curly hair just like her!* Layer on another poster. *Mother admires how she plays piano; I should practice until I can play just like her!* Layer on another poster over the last one. *All the teachers laugh at how funny she is; I need to be funnier just like her!* Layer yet another poster over all the others.

If, like me, you spent your formative years perfecting this game of poster plastering, you know the rules:

1. Find someone who's got what you need.

2. Be her.

See how much she's loved? Staple. *See how well she's accepted?* Staple. *See how easily she belongs?* Staple. Until you're nothing but a poster upon poster upon poster. And you feel like a poser, hiding your longing for belonging under a pile of façades.

When you've been told since earliest childhood that who you are is both "too much" and also "not enough," the only remaining option is to be everybody but yourself. Thus, the stapler.

Denise's Story

Days before my job interview, I sat at the kitchen table with my mom directly across from me. She asked me one question after another with her most professional sounding voice: *Why are you a good fit for this position? How would you handle a complaint from a customer? What are your strengths? What are your weaknesses?* Since my mom worked in human resources, she interviewed people all the time, so our time at the kitchen table was preparation for my upcoming interview.

I was 18 years old and had just graduated from high school. This new job would be my first real job outside of babysitting and working in the mall at Christmastime. I had carefully crafted my answers with her input, so I knew I would nail the real interview. But when our mock interview ended, my mom gave me one final piece of advice: *Just be yourself.* That one stumped me. Just be myself? How do I do that? What does that even mean?

Finding the Answer to Who We Really Are

We hear this advice all the time. If you're going on an interview, just be yourself. If you're going on a first date, just be yourself. If you're visiting your fiancé's parents for the first time, just be yourself. This kind of advice permeates the Internet as well: *Just be who you are. Be true to your authentic self.* But how do you do that if you're not entirely sure who the self is supposed to be? Ultimately, this kind of advice fails to deliver. When we try to define ourselves according to the world's labels, we come up short. Every time.

As we mentioned in the introduction of this book, both of us (Cheri and Denise) have spent considerable time learning the various personality frameworks. We can easily rattle off our Myers-Briggs type, our enneagram number, our top five strengths, and our preferred love language. Likewise, we can also launch into a lengthy discussion on what it means to be an HSP. All of these systems of thought provide a helpful language to understand common human experiences.

At the same time, while we find these different frameworks fascinating, true knowledge of self and the world can only come from God, the designer of this world and every person in it. While we are very grateful for Dr. Elaine Aron's research on Sensory Processing Sensitivity, we understand that no person can tell us *who* we are. Only God can do that. And he tells us in his Word who we are and why we are here. We are his beloved. Made in his image. God made each of us a unique creation, and we are here to glorify him.

The next time we hear the advice—just be yourself—we can know who that self really is. As believers in Christ, we are daughters of God. We are who he says we are. And the next time we are tempted to staple another person's identity over our own, we can remember that we don't have to do that anymore.

Weaknesses and Strengths

Even if you never had a mom "interview" you and ask you what your strengths and weaknesses are, you likely already have a good idea of what they might be. You know which settings drain you and which ones refill you. You know which activities you are not particularly well-suited for and which ones bring life and joy to your heart.

Discovering you're an HSP can be freeing in one sense. Learning about Sensory Processing Sensitivity helps to explain so many experiences that never made sense before. It also equips us with the knowledge we need to make proactive decisions in our relationships and our environments. Our hope throughout this entire book has been to demonstrate how HSPs do have certain sensitivities (which we often see as weaknesses), but they come with correlating strengths and we can harness those strengths to serve others. That's why we're here—to love God and love others—all for his glory.

We don't have to fret over any perceived frailties or sensitivities.

After all, God delights to use clay vessels that are not inherently strong in themselves. God chose stuttering Moses to lead a nation. God chose fearful Gideon to lead an army. God chose overlooked David to become a mighty king. God chose persecuting Paul to become a great evangelist and missionary. God's specialty is choosing the weak to overcome the strong. He chooses the foolish to teach the wise. He uses the lowly to surpass the great (1 Corinthians 1:25-31).

When we serve others from a place of weakness, something beautiful happens: We cannot take the credit. God gets all the glory. So, sometimes as HSPs, we may choose to serve in an area that is outside our comfort zones. That may mean serving food in a homeless shelter that is noisy and full of strangers. That may mean standing before a group of women, rather than an individual friend, to share our testimonies. That may mean going on a women's retreat to be a blessing to others, even if we think we'll return home exhausted.

We can serve in these ways knowing the toll they may take, but also knowing we can mitigate that toll in other ways. By understanding how we are wired, we can be proactive and prepare accordingly. Being sensitive to sensory overload does not mean we cannot serve others. It simply means we rely on God all the more. He is our strength. Today and always.

Notes

Introduction

1. Susan Cain, *Quiet: The Power of Introverts in a World That Can't Stop Talking* (New York, NY: Broadway Books, 2012), 102.

2. Ibid.

3. Ibid., 101.

4. Ibid., 133.

5. Elaine N. Aron, *The Highly Sensitive Person: How to Thrive When the World Overwhelms You* (New York, NY: Harmony Books, 1996), xxv.

Chapter 2—The Five Factors of Sensitivity

1. Elaine N. Aron, *The Highly Sensitive Person: How to Thrive When the World Overwhelms You* (New York, NY: Harmony Books, 1996), xvii-xxiii.

Chapter 3—The Five Fallacies of Sensitivity

1. Elaine N. Aron, *The Highly Sensitive Person: How to Thrive When the World Overwhelms You* (New York, NY: Harmony Books, 1996), xvii.

Chapter 4—The Way HSPs Are Wired

1. Susan Cain, *Quiet: The Power of Introverts in a World That Can't Stop Talking* (New York, NY: Broadway Books, 2012), 99-100.

2. Gregor Mendel, "Experiments in Plant Hybridization," read at the February 8th and March 8th, 1865, meetings of the Brünn Natural History Society, http://www.esp.org/foundations/genet-ics/classical/gm-65.pdf.

3. Kristen Hovet, "Sensory Overload: Some People Genetically Wired to Detest Bright Lights, Big Sounds," Genetic Literacy Project website, accessed March 11, 2019, https://geneticliteracypro ject.org/2017/10/10/sensory-overload-people-genetically-wired-detest-bright-lights-big-sounds/.

4. Cecilie L. Licht, Erik L. Mortensen, and Gitte M. Knudsen, "Association Between Sensory Processing Sensitivity and the 5-HTTLPR Short/Short Genotype," accessed March 11, 2019, doi: 10.1016/j.biopsych.2011.03.031.

Chapter 5—The Upside and the Downside

1. For more information, visit hsperson.com.

2. Seth Godin, *Tribes: We Need You to Lead Us* (New York, NY: Penguin Group, 2008), 2.

3. Ibid., 4.

4. C.S. Lewis, *The Four Loves* (New York, NY: Harcourt, 1960), 65.

5. Here's a brief sampling:

- Tanya Markul, "5 Superpowers of Highly Sensitive People," *From Struggle to Sparkle*, accessed January 10, 2019, http://thugunicorn.com/5-hsp/.
- Michaela Chung, "9 Superpowers of the Highly Sensitive Person," *Introvert Spring*, accessed January 10, 2019, https://introvertspring.com/9-superpowers-highly-sensitive-person/.
- Celeste O'Brien, "Your HSP Superpowers," *Authenticity Coaching for the Highly Sensitive Person*, accessed January 10, 2019, https://www.theauthentichsp.com/your-hsp-super-powers/.
- Leah Burkhart, "Five Super-Powers Introverts and Highly Sensitive People Possess," *The Healthy Sensitive*, accessed January 10, 2019, https://thehealthysensitive.com/2019/01/11/five-super-powers-introverts-and-highly-sensitive-people-possess/.
- David Master, "8 Highly Sensitive Person Super Powers," *DavidMasters.com*, accessed January 10, 2019, http://davidmmasters.com/blog/8-highly-sensitive-person-super-powers/.

6. Brittany Blount, "Being an HSP Is a Superpower—But It's Almost Impossible to Explain It," *Highly Sensitive Refuge*, accessed March 5, 2019, https://highlysensitiverefuge.com/highly-sensitive-person-hsp-superpower/.

7. Ibid.

8. Michaela Chung, "9 Superpowers of the Highly Sensitive Person," *Introvert Spring*, accessed January 10, 2019, https://introvertspring.com/9-superpowers-highly-sensitive-person/.

9. Kelly O'Laughlin, "HSP Podcast #10: HSP & Animals," *A Highly Sensitive Person's Life*, accessed February 22, 2019. http://highlysensitiveperson.net/episode10/.

Chapter 6—The Potential Pitfall for HSPs

1. Margot Bastin, Janne Vanhalst, Filip Raes, and Patricia Bijttebier, "Co-Brooding and Co-Reflection as Differential Predictors of Depressive Symptoms and Friendship Quality in Adolescents: Investigating the Moderating Role of Gender," *Journal of Youth and Adolescence* 47, no. 5 (May 2018): 1037-51, doi: 10.1007/s10964-017-0746-9.

2. Henry Cloud, *Boundaries for Leaders* (New York, NY: HarperCollins, 2013).

Chapter 7—The Difference Between Healthy and Unhealthy HSPs

1. This story is also shared in Cheri Gregory and Kathi Lipp's book *Overwhelmed* (Eugene, OR: Harvest House Publishers, 2017), 48-49.

2. Carol S. Dweck, *Mindset: The New Psychology of Success: How We Can Learn to Fulfill Our Potential* (New York, NY: Ballantine Books, 2008), 7.

3. Ibid., 6.

4. These diagrams are based on the work of David A. Kolb, *Experimental Learning: Experience as the Source of Learning and Development* (Englewood Cliffs, NJ: Prentice-Hall, 1984).

Chapter 8—The Good News about HSPs

1. Thomas Boyce, "Are you an orchid or a dandelion? This is one of the most important questions you'll ever answer," QuietRev.com, https://www.quietrev.com/are-you-an-orchid-or-a-dandelion-this-is-one-of-the-most-important-questions-youll-ever-answer (accessed March 19, 2019).

2. Michele Cushatt, "Undone Life Together: Week 4 Hot Topics," YouTube.com, https://www.youtube.com/watch?v=W6J7t7dXpUo (accessed March 19, 2019).

3. Thomas Boyce, "Are you an orchid or a dandelion? This is one of the most important questions you'll ever answer," QuietRev.com, https://www.quietrev.com/are-you-an-orchid-or-a-dande lion-this-is-one-of-the-most-important-questions-youll-ever-answer (accessed March 19, 2019).

4. Donna Jackson Nakazawa, *Childhood Disrupted: How Your Biography Becomes Your Biology, and How You Can Heal* (New York, NY: Atria Books, 2015), 75-80.

5. Thomas Boyce, "Are you an orchid or a dandelion? This is one of the most important questions you'll ever answer," QuietRev.com, https://www.quietrev.com/are-you-an-orchid-or-a-dande lion-this-is-one-of-the-most-important-questions-youll-ever-answer (accessed March 19, 2019).

Chapter 9—The Trouble with Bubble Baths

1. You can find the full articles here:

- Nikki Andersen, "20 Self-Care Ideas for Highly Sensitive People," Highly Sensitive Refuge, July 23, 2018, https://highlysensitiverefuge.com/self-care-ideas-for-highly-sensitive-people/.

- Amanda Kryska, "6 Daily Self-Care Rituals for Highly Sensitive People," Mind Body Green, accessed January 13, 2019, https://www.mindbodygreen.com/0-23283/6-daily-selfcare-ritu als-for-highly-sensitive-people.html.

- Renee Byrd, "43 Self-Care Practices for the Highly Sensitive Person", Will Frolic for Food, April 18, 2017, https://www.willfrolicforfood.com/blog/2017/04/43-self-care-practices-for-the-highly-sensitive-person.html.

2. Christianna Silva, "The Millennial Obsession with Self-Care," National Public Radio website, June 4, 2017, www.npr.org/2017/06/04/531051473/the-millennial-obsession-with-self-care.

3. Stephanie Kersta and Carolyn Plater, "The Wellness Program," Hoame website, accessed January 13, 2019, https://hoame.ca/corporate.

4. Stephanie Kersta, and Carolyn Plater, "The Dark Room," Hoame website, accessed January 13, 2019, https://hoame.ca/meditation/.

5. Yana Conner, "Questioning the Self-Care Movement," Intersect, October 24, 2018, http://inter sectproject.org/faith-and-work/questioning-self-care-movement/.

6. Andersen, "20 Self-Care Ideas for Highly Sensitive People."

7. Ibid.

8. Roni Loren, "Self-Care in Stressful Times for the Highly Sensitive Person (HSP)," Roni Loren website, accessed January 13, 2019, https://roniloren.com/blog/2017/2/15/self-care-in-stressful -times-for-the-highly-sensitive-person-hsp.

9. Acts 2:33, 7:55-56; Romans 8:34; Ephesians 1:20; Colossians 3:1; Hebrews 1:3, 8:1, 10:12, 12:2; 1 Peter 3:22; Revelation 3:21

Chapter 10—The Struggle with Stressful Situations

1. Rollo May, "Freedom and Responsibility Reexamined," *Behavioral Science and Guidance: Proposals and Perspectives*, edited by Esther Lloyd-Jones and Esther M. Westervelt (New York, NY: Teachers College, Columbia University, 1963), 103.

2. Danielle J. Maack, Erin Buchanan, and John Young. 2015. "Development and Psychometric Investigation of an Inventory to Assess Fight, Flight, and Freeze Tendencies: The Fight, Flight, Freeze Questionnaire." Cognitive Behavior Therapy 44 (2) (2015): 117-27. doi:10.1090/16506073.20 14.972443.

3. Pete Walker, "Codependency, Trauma and the Fawn Response," PeteWalker.com. http://pete -walker.com/codependencyFawnResponse.htm (retrieved December 29, 2018).

4. Bill Gaultiere, "Jesus Shows Us Healthy Relational Boundaries," Soul Shepherding. https://www .soulshepherding.org/jesus-shows-us-healthy-relational-boundaries (retrieved December 29, 2018).

Chapter 11—The Problem with Pretending

1. Trudy Ludwig, "Bullying Basics," TrudyLudwig.com. http://www.trudyludwig.com/author_bul lybasics.html (retrieved March 4, 2019).

Chapter 12—The Turmoil in Tender Hearts

1. Owen Strachan, "The Need for Hard Words in the Life of the Christian," Patheos website, accessed January 8, 2019, https://www.patheos.com/blogs/thoughtlife/2008/10/the-need-for -hard-words-in-the-life-of-the-christian/.

2. Ibid.

3. Ibid.

Chapter 13—The Enigma of Emotions

1. Rebecca Low, David Dyke, and Lauren Brown. "The Impact of a Digital Recorder Intervention in Pragmatic/Experiential Therapy for Couples: A Pilot Study to Assess Emotional Flooding." *Contemporary Family Therapy: An International Journal* 36 (1) (2014) : 70–82. doi:10.1007/ s10591-013-9259-1.

2. Andre Solo, "These 3 Uncommon Sets of Genes Make You a Highly Sensitive Person," Highly Sensitive Refuge, https://highlysensitiverefuge.com/highly-sensitive-person-gene (retrieved January 10, 2019).

3. Rebecca Todd, Mana Ehlers, Daniel J. Mueller, Amanda Robertson, Daniela Palombo, Natalie Free- man, Brian Levine, and Adam Anderson. (2015). "Neurogenetic Variations in Norepinephrine Availability Enhance Perceptual Vividness." *The Journal of Neuroscience* 35. 6506-16. 10.1523/ JNEUROSCI.4489-14.2015.

4. Douglas Stone and Sheila Heen. *Thanks for the Feedback: The Science and Art of Receiving Feedback Well,* (New York, NY: Penguin Books, 2015) 83-84.

5. This does not apply to relationships that involve Abuse, Addiction, Adultery, Apathy, or Abandon- ment. Such relationship issues are beyond the scope of this book and the guidance given here may backfire.

6. Elaine Aron, *The Highly Sensitive Person: How to Thrive When the World Overwhelms You* (New York, NY: Broadway Books, 1998), 51.

Chapter 15—The Weariness of Worship

1. Cain, *Quiet: The Power of Introverts in a World That Can't Stop Talking,* 66.

2. Ibid.

Chapter 16—The Complexity of Caring

1. B. P. Acevedo, E. N. Aron, A. Aron, M. Sangster, N. Collins, and L. L. Brown, (2014), "The highly sensitive brain: an fMRI study of sensory processing sensitivity and response to others' emotions." Brain Behav, 4: 580-594. doi:10.1002/brb3.242.

2. Ibid.

3. C. F. Alford, (2016) "Mirror Neurons, Psychoanalysis, and the Age of Empathy." *Int. J. Appl. Psychoanal. Studies*, 13: 7– 23. doi: 10.1002/aps.1411.

4. Andre Solo, "This is the Difference Between a Highly Sensitive Brain and a 'Typical' Brain," Highly Sensitive Refuge, https://highlysensitiverefuge.com/highly-sensitive-person-brain (retrieved January 5, 2019).

5. Anne L.C. Runehov, "Imago Dei and Simulatio or Imitatio Dei: A Philosophical Essay on Empathy," *Theology and Science*, Volume 10, Number 4 (November 2012), 411-430, http://ejournals.ebsco.com/direct.asp?ArticleID=4D3587606803F6532098, (retrieved March 13, 2019).

6. Brené Brown, *Rising Strong* (New York, NY: Spiegel & Grau, 2015), 114.

7. B. O. Olatunji, J. M. Lohr, & B. J. Bushman, (2007). "The pseudopsychology of venting in the treatment of anger: Implications and alternatives for mental health practice." In T. A. Cavell & K. T. Malcolm (Eds.), *Anger, aggression and interventions for interpersonal violence* (119-141). Mahwah, NJ, US: Lawrence Erlbaum Associates Publishers.

8. Jennifer Byrd-Craven, David C. Geary, Amanda J. Rose, Davide Ponzi, "Co-ruminating increases stress hormone levels in women," *Hormones and Behavior,* Volume 53, Issue 3, 2008, 489-492, http://www.sciencedirect.com/science/article/pii/S0018506X07002930 (retrieved March 15, 2019).

9. Brown, *Rising Strong*, 115.

Chapter 17—The Gift of Self-Forgetfulness

1. Timothy Keller, *The Freedom of Self-Forgetfulness: The Path to True Christian Joy* (Leyland, England: 10Publishing), 5.

2. Ibid., 32.

3. Ibid., 35.

4. Rick Warren, *The Purpose Drive Life: What on Earth Am I Here For?* (Grand Rapids, MI: Zondervan), entry for Day 19.

Chapter 18—The Gift of Time

1. Seth Godin, "Is it too little butter, or too much bread?" SethGodin.com, https://seths.blog/2015/12/is-it-too-little-butter-or-too-much-bread/ (retrieved December 30, 2015).

Chapter 19—The Gift of Service

1. Rick Warren, "Rick Warren to Pastors: Behind Every Ministry There Is Private Pain," Huffington Post website, accessed January 17, 2019, https://www.huffingtonpost.com/2014/06/11/rick-warren-ministry_n_5480409.html.

2. Frederick Buechner, "Vocation," *Wishful Thinking: A Theological ABC* (New York: Harper & Row, 1973), 95.

Chapter 20—The Gift of Listening

1. Elaine Aron, "Make Full Use of Your Sensitivity—Listening," The Highly Sensitive Person website, accessed January 16, 2019, http://hsperson.com/pages/2May10.htm.

2. "Luke the Historian: The Gospel of Luke," The Bible website, accessed January 16, 2019, https://bible.org/book/export/html/21296.

Chapter 22—The Gift of Creativity

1. Here's a brief sampling:

- Elaine Aron, "FAQ: Are Highly Sensitive People More Creative and Intelligent Than Other People?," The Highly Sensitive website, accessed January 15, 2019. https://hsperson.com/faq/are-hsps-more-creative-and-intelligent/.

- Carrie Brummer, "Are You a Highly Sensitive Creative?," Artist Strong website, accessed January 15, 2019, https://www.artiststrong.com/are-you-a-highly-sensitive-creative/.

- Douglas Eby, "Being Highly Sensitive and Creative," The Creative Mind website, accessed January 15, 2019, http://thecreativemind.net/126/being-highly-sensitive-and-creative/.

- Deborah Ward, "The Sensitive Mind Is a Creative Mind," Psychology Today website, accessed January 15, 2019, https://www.psychologytoday.com/us/blog/sense-and-sensitivity/201110/the-sensitive-mind-is-creative-mind.

2. Carolyn Gregoire, and Scott Barry Kaufman, *Wired to Create: Unraveling the Mysteries of the Creative Mind* (New York, NY: Perigee, 2015), 125.

3. Deborah Ward, "The Sensitive Mind Is a Creative Mind," Psychology Today website, accessed January 15, 2019, https://www.psychologytoday.com/us/blog/sense-and-sensitivity/201110/the-sensitive-mind-is-creative-mind.

4. Douglas Eby, "Being Highly Sensitive and Creative," The Creative Mind website, accessed January 15, 2019, http://thecreativemind.net/126/being-highly-sensitive-and-creative/.

5. Oswald Chambers, *My Utmost for His Highest* (Grand Rapids, MI: Discovery House, 1995), December 15 entry.

Chapter 23—The Gift of Influence

1. Susan Cain, *Quiet: The Power of Introverts in a World That Can't Stop Speaking.*

2. R. K. Greenleaf, *Servant Leadership:* (25th Anniversary ed.). (New York/Mahwah, NJ: Paulist Press), 27.

3. Adapted from Brian Tracy, "6 Qualities of a Charismatic Leader," Success.com, https://www.success.com/6-qualities-of-a-charismatic-leader/ (retrieved 02/03/19).

4. Adapted from Dirk van Dierendonck, "Servant Leadership: A Review and Synthesis." *Journal of Management* 37, no. 4 (July 2011): 1228–61. doi:10.1177/0149206310380462.

5. D. Goleman, (1998). "What Makes a Leader?" *Harvard Business Review,* 76, 93-102.

6. John C. Maxwell, *The 21 Irrefutable Laws of Leadership: Follow Them and People Will Follow You* (Nashville, TN: Thomas Nelson), 13.

Acknowledgments

Denise would like to thank:

My HSP writing partner and friend, Cheri. This book would not have come to fruition without your foresight and ingenuity. You are the passionate force behind this book, while I have happily come along for the ride. You have been a joy and a delight to work with on this project. Thank you for asking. I will forever be a reluctant HSP, but you make me braver in this collection of narratives and this constellation of sensitivities.

Our editor, Kathleen. You have championed this project from the beginning, and there isn't anyone with whom we would rather have taken this journey than you.

Our agent, Steve. Thank you for believing in us and in this book.

My HSP and non-HSP children. You know better than anyone that sensitivity is not synonymous with timidity, because I love each of you fiercely.

My non-HSP husband, Jeff. I'm pretty sure you figured out I was an HSP long before either of us knew it was "a thing." You are the first and only person ever to call me your "princess who could always find the pea." Thank you for loving me with all my sensitive and strong proclivities.

My HPS (Highly Perfect Savior), Jesus. I have no idea what your human DNA might have been, but I am convinced you were the fullness of both God and man. You are the perfect wholeness of everything it means to be both sensitive and strong. Thank you for creating me as I am, and thank you for being the great I AM.

Cheri would like to thank:

Denise Hughes, for your friendship and leadership. It has been a blast delighting in our similarities and hashing out our differences. I can't imagine this book—or my life—without your research, experience, wisdom, and passion for truth. You are my Proverbs 27:17—iron, constantly challenging me to go deeper into the Word. You are also one of my all-time favorite writers, which means I've spent the past year pinching myself and bragging to my mirror: I'm writing a book with *Denise Hughes*!

Kathi Lipp, for not merely tolerating but actively championing my HSP-ity for over a decade now. Thank you for creating such safe spaces for me to grow strong. (As for the *dozen roses* you sent when Denise and I signed this contract? Your generosity flat-out amazes and inspires me. Always.)

Amy Carroll, my reflective life-processing partner. I love your tender heart and strong voice...and how you always get choked up when you talk about Jesus.

Michele Cushatt, my HSP soul-sister and lifeline. I love your relentless search for truth, regardless of cost. Your gift of affirming while prodding is priceless.

Kendra Burrows, Shantell Brightman, and Cheri Fletcher, my sensitive and strong noticers and caregivers. I don't know what I'd do without you!

Emily Freeman and the amazing women of The Artist's Bench—Angela, Anjuli, Erin, Marian, Melissa, Meredith, Kamille, and Shaina—for buoying me through rejection and encouraging me to plant the seeds that grew into this book.

Kathleen Kerr, for a long talk at Starbucks, a short talk at Leverage, and every single email and text message. The way you listen until you understand and then build on what you've heard blesses me and blows me away.

Steve Laube, for seeing the need for this book five years ago and patiently supporting me through the journey God knew I needed to take before I'd be ready to write it.

Annemarie and Jonathon, I love your sensitive hearts and strong convictions.

Daniel, for 30-plus years, you're the one person who gets me, even when my brand of HSP looks nothing like yours. Thank you for always supporting me in looking in, looking up, and looking out. You're my favoritest Highly Sensitive Husband.

Jesus, thank you for rescuing me, delighting in me, and being the Strength of this tender heart.

About the Authors

About Denise J. Hughes:

A teacher at heart, Denise loves the world of words, where life and literature connect, but she's most passionate about the book with living words—the Word of God. Denise is the author of *Deeper Waters: Immersed in the Life-Changing Truth of God's Word* (2017, Harvest House), and she's the General Editor of the *CSB (in)courage Devotional Bible* (2018, B&H). In addition to leading a weekly Bible study at her church, Denise enjoys speaking at conferences, retreats, and other women's events. She enjoys writing for the First 5 app by Proverbs 31 Ministries, and she always looks forward to those moments she can be in the classroom, teaching English. Denise holds a BA in Human Development, an MA in English, and she is currently pursuing a Master of Divinity at Gateway Seminary. She lives in Southern California with her husband and three kids, where she always finds times for peach tea, old books, and a good football game.

Her website: DeniseJHughes.com

Instagram: @DeniseJHughes

Facebook: @DeniseJHughes

About Cheri Gregory:

Through Scripture and storytelling, Cheri loves sharing experiences that connect to women's frustrations, fears, and failures, giving them hope that they are not alone—that someone gets them. She delights in helping women draw closer to Jesus, the strength of every tender heart. Cheri is the coauthor, with Kathi Lipp, of *You Don't Have to Try So Hard* and *Overwhelmed*. She's also the cohost, with Amy Carroll, of the Grit 'n' Grace podcast.

Cheri serves as the curriculum director and alumni coordinator for

The LEVERAGE Speaker Conference and loves speaking for women's events, especially weekend retreats.

Cheri holds a BA in English, an MA in Leadership. She teaches AP English Literature and Composition at a small Christian boarding school and is working on a PhD in Leadership, researching the leadership journeys of influential Christian women bloggers. She's been married to Daniel, her college sweetheart, for thirty years. The Gregorys have two adult children and live on the central California coast.

Her website: CheriGregory.com

Facebook: @Cheri.Gregory.Author

Instagram: @cheri_gregory

Books by Denise J. Hughes

6 Stories Every Mom Should Tell

Create a keepsake your children will treasure when you use this beautiful journal to share 6 of the most important stories a mom could tell, stories that shape who your children are, who they will become, and give them a window into your heart.

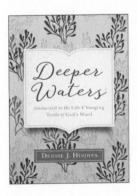

Deeper Waters

Do you come to God's Word with doubts that arise from life's disappointments? Denise J. Hughes has been there, yet she's found a peace that runs deeper than her circumstances. Discover a joy you never thought possible when reading the Bible.

Word Writers® Series

Join Denise J. Hughes as she guides you through the Word Writers Bible study series. As you explore Ephesians using this thoughtful and meaningful method, you will daily read God's Word, reflect on its meaning, respond with personal application, and practice Scripture memory.

Word Writers® Ephesians

The book of Ephesians examines relationships and how they matter to a life lived in Christ.

Word Writers® Philippians

The book of Philippians reminds you to be pure, true, and holy while not being anxious about anything.

Word Writers® James

The book of James calls you to grow deeper in your faith through words and actions as you look ahead to eternity with God and His people. Get ready to explore this stirring book through the tried-and-tested inductive study method—with an added writing step to help you treasure each word!

Books by Cheri Gregory

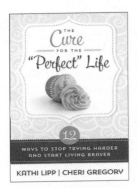

The Cure for the Perfect Life
(coauthored with Kathi Lipp)

Do you feel like you fall short of being the wife, mother, daughter, and friend you long to be? This self-help guide offers girlfriend-to-girlfriend empathy and experience that will help you tell the difference between reasonable rules and bad ones and discover biblical wisdom to overcome the bad rules in your life.

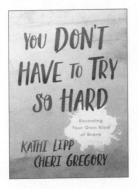

You Don't Have to Try So Hard
(coauthored with Kathi Lipp)

Are you daily struggling to meet impossible standards? You don't have to be a slave to perfectionism and people-pleasing! Use this guide to ditch your feelings of inadequacy and come face-to-face with the bold, balanced woman God created you to be.

Proverbs 31
MINISTRIES

About Proverbs 31 Ministries

If you were inspired by this book and desire to deepen your own personal relationship with Jesus Christ, Denise encourages you to connect with Proverbs 31 Ministries.

Proverbs 31 Ministries exists to be a trusted friend who will take you by the hand and walk by your side, leading you one step closer to the heart of God through:

- *Encouragement for Today* daily devotions
- First 5 Bible study app
- Online Bible Studies
- Podcast
- COMPEL Writer Training
- She Speaks Conference
- Books and resources

For more information about Proverbs 31 Ministries, visit: www.Proverbs31.org.